SUNNYSIDE MEMORIES

by

Paul Turner

Published and distributed by:
Village Marketing,
145 W 400 North Richfield, Utah 84701.
Phone: 1-800-982-6683
Suggested Retail: $13.00 (Please add S&H $3.00)

Cover Picture: Mother's shadow indicated we're facing the right direction for one of her many pictures. Frank Nuzio has just purchased their family Sunday dinner from us. Sister Ella Ruth and Vera Nuzio in back. Little brother Grant and me in front. Photo author's collection.

ISBN: 1-57636-049-0
Library of Congress Catalog Card Number: 97-62295
Production by: *SunRise Publishing, Orem, Utah*

To Mother & Dad
Everyone needs a Sunnyside in his life.

ABOUT THE AUTHOR

Paul Turner was born in 1931 in Sunnyside and lived there until 1951. He and his wife, Ardyth Gibson Turner, formerly of Dragerton, are the parents of nine children and forty plus grandchildren.

This is Turner's first experience as a writer, and his greatest fear is that he will be cited for practicing history without a license.

The Bend in the Road

Sometimes we come to life's crossroads
and view what we think is the end,
But God has a much wider vision,
and He knows it's only a bend.
The road will go on and get smoother,
and after we've stopped for a rest,
The path that lies beyond us
is often the part that is best...

So rest and relax and grow stronger
let go and let God share your load,
And have faith in a brighter tomorrow,
you've just come to a bend in the road.

—*Helen Steiner Rice*

SPECIAL THANKS

To my sister, Ella Ruth, who, after my third Sunnyside Memories story for our family newsletter said, "Keep writing, we're going to publish." Was she out of her mind?

Because she is my older sister, I obeyed her as a youngster and thought it the prudent thing to do now. Besides, her teaching, editing and English skills made my writing readable. I wrote, she corrected, and we published.
Thanks E.R.

Key to Photo Abbreviations
GEA   George Edward Anderson. Most early photographs dating back to the late 1890s to early 1900s were taken by Anderson. In some cases present owners of these photographs will also be acknowledged.
HBLL-BYU   Photographic Archives, Harold B. Lee Library, Brigham Young University.
USHS   Utah State Historical Society.
WM&RM   Western Mining and Railroad Museum.

PROLOGUE

Basking in the reflected joy of Utah's Centennial celebrations, my memories were activated as Ardyth and I drove to the Sunnyside Annual Reunion. As I grow older these encounters with the past bring a smile to my spirit. I remember how, as a youngster with mother, her eyes would light up when we encountered someone from her hometown. Funny how history repeats itself.

The reunion was great. We visited with a multitude of former Sunnysiders who had come for the festivities. We spent over three hours reminiscing about the town, the barn, the company mules, the school, the store and much more.

Jeanine Gilligan and I discussed how each of our families had lived in the house by the barn when our dads took care of the mine animals. As others joined in the discussion, I was brought back clearly to the time I wandered into the blacksmith and leather shop by the creek across from our house, and dad and a mule were doing battle. My memory still reverberates with the powerful scriptures my young ears heard quoted that day.

Duane Soderquist told of the times he played the trombone, John Preston played the fiddle and my brother, Dean, played the trumpet for the town dances. "We had a lot of fun and one night we made ten bucks." They split the money three ways. Every cent was welcome in those early days.

As we visited with Amel and Taylor Dennison I remembered, as a young boy, going uptown for Amel's wedding shivaree. Amel remembered that day, too. In the 1930s, when a couple married, all the kids in town gathered in front of the house where the newly-weds were staying to bang on cans and pans and make a loud racket and eat the candy that had been bought for the occasion. I related to him how impressed I was with the containers of candy waiting for us on the piano bench in his parent's house. I had never seen that much candy before. I was sold on shivarees.

One person clearly remembered, all these years later, having mother as his fourth-grade teacher. "Too many children don't have teachers like your mother. She not only taught in the classroom, but she would also work with us in the lunch room during the noon hour. She was a one-of-a-kind teacher." Other former students concurred. I agreed.

When Ollie Lindsay brought out his group pictures of area coal miners in the 1940s and 1950s, Jimmy Eaquinto could identify every one. Between the two of them they remembered all the Sunnysiders from those years and beyond.

Our final visit was with Kendall Nelson. He grew up with Grant and me and was Grant's age. We got a good laugh over an incident that I had completely forgotten. He said that he and I had just left the bowling alley in Sunnydale and were headed home. I was in dad's new 1950 Chev pickup. Kendall was in his 1939 Chev coupe. We were racing up Sunnydale's main street (of course I find this very hard to believe). I had the lead and as Kendall tried to pass me, another car pulled out from the opposite direction into his lane. Kendall swerved, losing control of his car. His car slid across a front lawn, hitting the front porch supports of the house. The porch roof came crashing down as he finally skidded to a stop on the driveway between the house and the garage.

When deputy marshals, Charlie Campagni, arrived and began asking questions, Kendall explained that he had reached for something on the floor and lost control Since Charlie's nephew was a passenger in Kendall's car, it helped give his story veracity. Deputy Charlie said, "Pay for the porch and slow down and there will be no ticket this time. In the meantime, I drove innocently home not even aware that anything had happened. These days I use the rearview mirror more. Kendall's car suffered a broken headlight and a few scratches which we both agreed was a small price to pay.

At the end of that memorable day, Ardyth and I gathered up our pictures, histories and scrapbooks and said our good-byes. We took a quick detour through the area of old Sunnyside and on up the canyon to the remains of the asphalt quarry. We got out and walked around while I related to her my experiences working for the asphalt company.

As we got back in the car and headed for home, warns Sunnyside memories continued to circulate in our thoughts.

Writing Reasons

There were two reasons for writing this memory book. The first was for an old man to share memories with his kids, grandkids, and others who may enjoy reading about growing up in small town America during the 1930s and 40s.

The second reason for writing? Read the book and I'll share the second reason with you on the last page.

One of the first homes in Sunnyside—1897 (Photo Courtesy WM&RM)

When the mines began opening in Carbon County in the late 1870's and the railroad was built, people began to immigrate to the West from Europe, Asia and Mexico. There were and still are about 27 different ethnic groups in Carbon County. The largest groups from the mining immigrants are the Italians, Greeks and Slovenians. The Mormon Pioneers had already settled this area, as farmers, and when the mines opened many of them worked in the mines to supplement their farm income.

PROLOGUE TWO

Jefferson Tidwell was a frontier entrepreneur. After arriving in the Utah Territory his colonization efforts included three counties. He first settled in Sanpete County. LDS Church President Brigham Young had expressed interest as early as 1875 in "the lands east of Sanpete" as a possible site for colonization.

In June of 1877 a party of five men, including Jefferson Tidwell, was sent to Castle Valley to investigate possible sites for settlement.

By 1896, Jefferson Tidwell of Wellington took title to some land at the mouth of Whitmore Canyon, twenty-five miles east of Price, and with his three sons began working the coal seam there.

In a 1908 coal-fraud case we learn more about this far-sighted pioneer who unhesitatingly looked for opportunity over the next horizon.

MARCH & APRIL, 1908 73 year old JEFFERSON TIDWELL (testimony in coal-fraud cases) Spinning his yarn about Sunnyside coal, "It stuck out six or seven feet high and rods across, and in the sun of a bright morning it glittered like silver. I was poor, we were all poor, so it looked awfully good to us. We dug and drilled and worked until we were out of food, and our feet were out of our shoes. We did the best we knew how. We were on unsurveyed ground so held it by work." p 131 NECESSARY FRAUD by Nancy J. Taniguchi 1996.
(Photo Courtesy GEA—HBLL—BYU)

TABLE OF CONTENTS

AUGUST THAWS

August is my favorite month. It thaws in August. I was born in March in Sunnyside, Utah. I was born during a cold month in a cold town. I'm cold blooded. People born in August are warm blooded. My wife was born in August. Her blood is three degrees warmer than mine. Our thermostat will verify this.

Sunnyside is in a canyon. Canyon towns are cold towns unless it is a canyon town down south. Sunnyside is up north. Before the doctor gave me my first spanking so I could get a breath of cold air, he asked my mom how come I had goose bumps. She replied, "I guess he's cold." My mom was very perceptive. She recognized my problem early on. I got the spanking anyway.

A canyon town is surrounded by mountains. When I was a kid in Sunnyside the sun came up about ten in the morning and set about three in the afternoon. And that was when the days were the longest. During winter, some days the sun was not up long enough to see it. Without a lot of sun a town becomes a cold town. I liked Sunnyside a lot but it was a cold town and I am cold blooded.

After my first birthday our family moved to a house at the mouth of the canyon so my dad could have a steady job at the coal mine. Sunnyside is a coal mining town. Our new house was out in the open. At the mouth of the canyon the wind attacks with more vim and vigor. In August the wind is warm. I like August.

I had a favorite spot in our new house. Well, two places really, because we had two stoves. Cold blooded people like stoves. Especially if they have a raging fire in them.

In our front room—they call them living rooms now—

was a pot bellied stove in the corner. The stove stood out from the corner about eighteen inches. Curling around behind that stove in the corner, lying on the floor, was my favorite spot. Sometimes that corner could get awfully hot. But for me, the hotter the better. Cold blooded people like hot places. Just thinking about it now can warm my blood by at least two degrees.

Shortly after our move there, dad arrived home from a trip to the D.T.R. Furniture store in Price with a new "Warm Morning Heater" for that corner. It was now called a heater, not a stove. That's what technology in the 1930s could do for you.

The new heater had a place on the back where you poured in water. Moisture, or vapor, would drift into the room and supposedly make it easier to breathe. At least that's how it was explained to me but I never did get it. Cold air is cold air no matter how much water or vapor gets involved. The only warm spot in that room was next to that heater. Homes now have insulation, but the only insulation we had back then was that stuff wrapped around the two wires hanging down from the center of the ceiling holding the light globe.

One of my jobs as a kid was to pour water into the receptacle on the back of the heater. I never could see that it did any good, but when I missed the receptacle and hit the firebox with the water—now that's what I call vapor, sizzling vapor. My older brothers and sisters would yell at me for missing the mark but the sizzle and column of steam rising clear to the ceiling was worth the verbal abuse. Most of my spare time during the cold months was spent curled up behind that "Warm Morning Heater."

We also had a stove in the kitchen. It was an old Monarch Range. A kitchen stove was called a Range, but I still called it a stove. It had a broken temperature gauge on the oven door. The gauge was not important because I knew whether or not it had a fire in it. Cold blooded people don't need gauges, they need heat.

My mother was a good cook. I ate a lot so she would cook more. When she cooked I knew there would be a hot fire. Cold blooded people can also be bright.

We had a little brother, Grant. He was born in September. He didn't spend as much time around the stoves as I did. He was probably warm blooded. Then again, with seven kids in our family, maybe there was no more room around the stoves.

Grant and I chopped wood and hauled in the wood and coal used in those two stoves. Those chores were not some of my favorites, but I was prompt for survival reasons. Cold blooded people know their priorities. When dad decided to build a fire, fuel was one thing I didn't want him worrying about.

Mother would read to us each night at bedtime. She would bring a chair by the stove and put her feet in the oven to keep warm. Mother was born in July. She was either the exception to my theory or she was building my self esteem by showing me that she liked the heat, too. Mother was like that—her kids' esteem came before her own comfort.

The kitchen stove also heated a hot water tank standing next to it. When space around the stoves was taken, I'd stand with my back against the tank searching for a little heat. Saturday was bath day so the tank turned cold by late afternoon.

As I got older I learned about a guy named Sam McGee. You probably remember him from your junior high school literature class. The poem is called, "The Cremation of Sam McGee." I learned about this old whippersnapper who left the south for Alaska. He froze to death. They can't dig graves in frozen ground so they put him in a furnace to cremate his remains. When they opened the furnace door later, old Sam was smiling and said that this was the first time he had been warm since he left—now get this—Tennessee. You want my theories confirmed? Then listen up. Sam and my dad's family were both from Tennessee. Sam is probably a cousin of ours, and Sam probably was born in the winter. Those are two theories that don't need facts. See what I mean? Talk about heredity AND environment. I got cold blood from both. No wonder I can't win. Well, so much for theories.

The way to solve all of this in a perfect world is to have all of the cold blooded folks work in the jungles of Panama building a new canal, and have all of the warm blooded people work the oil fields on Alaska's North Slope. Those with spring and fall birthdays could just go to—wherever they want to find work. Just an idea for biologists to consider . . .

I could also solve most of Washington's problems if they would just call me. Now you know why August is my favorite month.

Panoramic View of Sunnyside. (Photo courtesy of GEA-HBLL-BYU)

SUNNYSIDE

In 1896 Jefferson Tidwell of Wellington took title to some land at the mouth of Whitmore Canyon, twenty-five miles east of Price, Utah. Tidwell and his three sons began working the coal seam there. Two years later Utah Fuel Company bought the rights to the property and soon the railroad line was extended to Sunnyside. At the turn of the century houses began to be constructed for the miners and their families who were then living in tents. Some of the first houses built for the mine supervisors and managers were five rooms with an indoor bathroom. The rest of the houses had four rooms and outdoor toilets. The Company owned all of them.

Coke ovens were soon built below town and by 1918, at the height of World War I, the population of Sunnyside reached nearly 3,000 people. At this time it took about 2500 tons of coal per day to keep the ovens running seven days a week. After the war ended, coal mining and coke production dwindled until during the Depression, work at the mine was reduced to three days a week and the coke ovens operation shut down completely. Sunnyside reached its lowest point in 1933 when the mine employed a total of forty-six men. A complete shutdown was prevented when war again broke out in Europe and in 1938 an additional twenty men were hired to increase production and reclaim and clean up the mine. After the bombing of Pearl Harbor in 1941 the Sunnyside mine and coke ovens were once again activated and the second population boom in the area began.

An L.D.S. church was built in 1900 and was also used as the first public school for a year until a school was built. The only toilet facilities for either building were the customary outhouses.

A general store and butcher shop, owned and operated by the mining company, were built in the center of town. The mining company issued scrip which could be drawn in advance of payday and used to buy merchandise at these company owned places of business only. If traded for cash, the exchange was eighty cents cash for one dollar scrip. Many miners became perpetually indebted through these transactions.

During the boom years of World War I, a lighthouse was built high on the mountain overlooking the tipple. The huge light was rolled out on tracks to the front of this small enclosure to light the payroll truck as it traveled from Price to the mine office in Sunnyside. The light was no longer needed during the Depression and eventually was destroyed. But the lighthouse, itself, continued to be used by the children of Sunnyside to fill their adventure fantasies. It still stands, a lonely sentinel, guarding an empty valley.

An amusement hall was built near the store and mine office and was used at various times for programs, dances, graduation exercises and a theatre. The basement contained a pool hall, confectionery and, during the early 1940s, a teen dance area, complete with jukebox.

During World War II the mining company built a completely new subdivision below Sunnyside. It was called Sunnydale. A new store was built there in 1944. It was operated by the Price Trading Company. A movie theatre was included in the building and the basement contained a bowling alley, barber shop and snack bar.

The old Sunnyside store was torn down and the amusement hall was repaired and used as a boarding house for single men who came to the mines to work.

Additional seams of coal were mined and Sunnyside continued to grow. The Number Four mine had been classified as a non-gassy mine, but in 1943 methane gas was detected in its tunnels. This was new to most of the miners and they had to be trained and educated on the dangers of this gas and the use of flame safety lamps.

When the Allies were victorious in Europe, V.E. Day was proclaimed across the country. The mines in Sunnyside were idled for a one day celebration. The next day, May 9, 1945, the day shift totalling eighty-five men was preparing to come out of the Number Four mine. At 3:12 p.m. the methane gas in the mine was somehow ignited. A violent explosion rocked the mine. After three days of struggle by combined mine rescue crews from all around Carbon County, the death toll totalled twenty-three miners who ranged in age from twenty-three to seventy-three years. It was a sorrowful time for everyone in Sunnyside.

With the expansion of underground mining tunnels, the danger to the original townsite of Sunnyside grew. Two new schools were built in Sunnydale, as well as a new L.D.S. chapel. The mining company decided to vacate all the original Sunnyside houses, so began moving the residents into empty houses in Sunnydale. The old mine office and amusement hall were demolished and the remaining vacant houses were sold to individual buyers and removed. With the end of World War II, eventually all coal shipments from Sunnyside were halted and the mine was idled indefinitely.

The town of Sunnydale was re-named Sunnyside and the mining operations were sold to the Sunnyside Reclamation Company in the late 1980s. The old tipple was eventually torn down and replaced with a new building further south. By 1991 the new mining company was supplying coal to the Geneva Steel Plant in Orem which had re-opened after a two year closure.

Asphalt milling in Sunnyside began in 1890. In 1892,

Richards Street in Salt Lake City was paved with rock asphalt from the Sunnyside deposit. This spurred interest in rock asphalt for paving purposes and for several years was the main material used in paving. However, production of rock asphalt was costly and time consuming. Asphalt operations in Sunnyside were worked sporadically by struggling companies through the early years of this century. In 1927 a Colorado company tried to develop a successful operation. They spent nearly a half million dollars equipping the operation with adequate machinery, including a three and a half mile aerial tram in the canyon above town, but they were not successful in selling sufficient tonnage to warrant continuing the operation and went bankrupt in 1931. In 1932 the Rock Asphalt Company of Utah took over the plant and were able to operate it on a successful commercial basis only intermittently. But with the development of other less costly paving materials, the cost of producing rock asphalt for paving outweighed the financial return and eventually the asphalt mill in Sunnyside closed for good.

Only the main town bridge, lighthouse on the mountain and a few crumbling steps on Goblers Knob are left to indicate that the original townsite was twice a flourishing coal mining town called Sunnyside.

The evolution, including the birth and death of old Sunnyside.
(Photos courtesy GEA-USHS)

From near the Light House on the mountain the apartments (bottom left) and the "Jap" Hotel (center) dominate Lower Town. (Photo courtesy John C. Preston)

A BED IN EVERY ROOM

I own a moving company so I'm in and out of houses all over the country. I've seen some fairly humble homes and I've seen some that resemble small hotels in size and opulence. I have moved furniture for people who live in one bedroom apartments and others who live in six and eight bedroom mansions.

Not long ago, when I commented on the spacious size of the rooms I was carrying furniture into, someone asked me about the house I grew up in. I answered, "Why, I grew up in a four bedroom house." Then I laughed and added, "it only had four rooms total but when I was young there was a bed in every room."

In remembering that little less than five hundred square feet, four room cement and coke breeze house in Sunnyside, I wonder now how my parents managed to put seven people in such a small area.

The first bed I remember being in was the crib in the northeast room during a Christmas Eve visit from Santa. I must have been a little over a year and a half old. I remember being scared of Santa and crying. In that same eight feet by ten feet room was a piano and a double bed where my two sisters, Winifred and Ella Ruth, slept. This room had a wide arch in the wall connecting it to the front room.

The next bed I remember was in the only real bedroom in the house which we called "the back bedroom" in the northeast corner of the house. This was my parents' bedroom. It was ten feet by twelve feet and held two double beds, two chests of drawers and a trunk. Dad and mother slept in one bed and my brothers, Ned and Clair, and I slept in the other one. I slept between my brothers and was NOT TO TOUCH either of them as their backs were turned to me. Talk about a tough assignment!

Little brother, Grant, had outgrown the bassinet and slept in the baby crib I had outgrown. By this time oldest brother, Dean, was going to school in Provo, so slept on the front room couch when he came home. The two small closets in the wall between the northeast room and the northwest bedroom were about two feet deep and three feet wide which was, actually, adequate space for our few clothes.

Sometime later a one room "shack" was purchased by mother and dad and placed next to the northwest outer wall of the house. This eight feet by six feet wooden frame room (no insulation, no heat) became sleeping quarters for Ned and Clair. It was just wide enough for a double bed and whatever fabulous treasures (junk) they could find to store for later use. When the wind blew hard enough it blew the door open. In the winter the snow blew in through the cracks around the window and under the door. They always woke up to snowflakes on their bed and by the door after a storm. When they moved out into this "private" bedroom, Grant and I moved into the other bed in our parents' bedroom for the next few years.

All our beds were double, with worn mattresses on top of squeaky springs which made every mattress sag in the middle. Staying on your own side of the bed took skill and practice.

During my growing up years, we had two stretches of time when we lived in our newly constructed home in Provo, each stretch lasting two years. My beds there were located in the basement bedroom, the basement fruit room, and a cot in the kitchen by the south windows. It was in the kitchen bed that mother kissed my forehead at daylight August 10, 1941 and whispered that Ned had been killed in a car accident. It was a sad time.

We moved back to Sunnyside a few weeks later. By then, Dean was married and living in Provo and Winifred was married and living in Salt Lake. So Ella Ruth's bed became the front room couch which had to be made up with quilts and a pillow each morning and night, and Grant and I moved into the northeast room.

In the summers Grant and I slept in a double bed out on the front porch. More than one night we lay very still as drunken men passed our house coming from the pool hall and going to their homes in lower town. Sometimes they came alone and sometimes in pairs, arguing all the way.

The "shack" had been sold and a new back porch built onto the back of the house. During these years World War II was being fought, Clair was in the Army, Dean's wife had died and he was in the Service, so his two children, Bob and Deanna, came to live with us. Winifred's husband was overseas with the Air Force and she and her baby daughter, Dianne, came home to live, too.

Ella Ruth continued to sleep on the front room couch. When winter came the new back porch became the bedroom for Grant and me. It was bitter cold (no heat and no insulation again) and I remember the two of us discussing, tongue in cheek, whether we would perish by freezing or being crushed to death under the load of heavy quilts mother kept piling on us. I was in the back porch bed when mother kissed my forehead and said that our cousin, Wade, had been killed in an accident with a coal-filled railroad car. This was another sad time for our family.

As I watch my children and grandchildren with their own carpeted, individual bedrooms equipped with TVs, VCRs, big closets crammed with clothes, desks, etc. I remember all too well "the good old days." I'll take modern bedrooms with their light switches and thermostats any day.

And yet, I'll always remember that little crowded house that was so full of love and enjoyment that we never realized then that we were poor or deprived. What we lacked in space we made up for in fun and excitement. I don't want to go back to those old days, but I'll never forget them, either.

Mother and dad in the 1920s with my older brother Dean and sister Winifred.

Our home in Sunnyside just north of the Barn. The outhouse, coal shed and bath tub hanging on the back porch are clearly visible as is our "solar dryer" with clothes hanging from the clothes line.

THE AMUSEMENT HALL

Before TV and malt shops came along we went to the movies and stopped at the counter of an ice cream parlor where, like the movies, you had to go inside to get what you wanted. My favorite was always a thick chocolate malt. These days we sometimes go for a drive and stop at the drive-in window for a shake. I've heard chocolate fills veins with cholesterol faster than vanilla does, so I always get vanilla now. I'm not sure they've got this cholesterol thing pegged right anyway. What if I give up chocolate completely and they find out after I'm dead that it was something else that elevates cholesterol? You remember a few years ago that scare with cranberries, then apples and recently, strawberries. What will they think of next?

In old Sunnyside the store, mine office and amusement hall were built in the early 1900s. The amusement hall, complete with pool hall and large multipurpose room, was completed in 1915. These early buildings were built before the First World War when the coal mines were doing well and miners needed somewhere to pick up their paychecks and quickly spend them. And their families needed a place for dances, programs and a place to enjoy an early silent movie when one could be procured.

By the 1930s, in the midst of the depression, the store and office continued to operate but the amusement hall closed down, the school gym was used for dances and programs and we went to Columbia or Price for our movies. I'm not sure the pool hall ever closed down, though.

During World War II the demand for coal and coke increased as part of the war effort and the amusement hall opened again with a new confectionery in the basement and a movie theater upstairs complete with slanted floor and real, bolted down theater seats. During this time a different movie was shown each week. The talkies had arrived but the films were still in black and white. When technicolor made its debut everyone was astonished at the bright array of colors. Children got in for a dime and adults paid twenty-five cents. Ella Ruth was the cashier and remembers fondly the elegant Mrs. Yarnell, the manager for a couple of years, who taught her some of the finer points of social etiquette.

The confectionery was a neat place to hang out. In the beginning they had a slot machine (the kind of one-armed bandit that fills Las Vegas casinos). It was a nickel machine. I remember it well. Youngsters were not to play it and we were youngsters. But no one enforced the age limit because the machine, itself, was against the law.

One day Louis Rossi, Martin Rodosh and I were drinking malts at the counter. The machine was setting right in front of us. Louis said, "Let's each put in ten cents and we'll be partners and split any winnings." We each gave our two nickels to Martin and on the third nickel he hit the jackpot and the nickels began flowing out the front of that machine. We were stuffing our pockets with nickels when manager, Roxie Boggs, came out of the back room. She saw what was happening and said, "You boys are too young to play that machine. Now go on home before I call the Marshall." We took our pockets full of nickels out to the front lawn and divided up the loot evenly. I don't remember ever playing that machine again but we did have good luck that one time.

Some time later the Marshall made the confectionery folks get rid of the slot machine. But he approved a non-paying pin-ball machine. The first pin-ball machine would give winners free games. Some of the older players could get the ball moving just slow enough to stop on one of the winning chutes. Then, with a slight bump on the front of the machine, the free games would add up. Each guy would play for about an hour and then change off and another would play. When the free games got low the current player, using some skill, would get the ball to hang up and the free game would continue. That's the only pin-ball machine that ever lost money for its owner.

The outside of the amusement hall was a unique place to play for Sunnyside youngsters. There was a ten inch ledge between the first and second floors. You could climb the stairs on either the north or south side of the building and get onto the ledge, then work your way around to the front porch and steps. It was about a twelve feet drop and scary but I don't remember anyone ever falling off. There was no slippery slide in town but the covering for the furnace room steps was made of cement and we made that do when we wanted to slide. The bigger kids could run up that cement cover and get to the ledge. I remember the first day I could run fast enough, keeping the momentum going, to just catch the ledge and hang on. It had taken all the stamina I had so I slid back down that day rather than walk the ledge.

When the town officials put up the large Christmas tree on the front lawn of the amusement hall that year, we had another great obstacle for our game of tag. With our tag game we could stay out of the way of the one designated "It" by running up the stairs, walking the ledge, climbing the Christmas tree and dropping off the branches opposite where "It" was climbing. Or the big boys could hang down from the ledge, dropping the distance to the ground. Most of the boys in town gathered for games at the amusement hall when their chores were finished in the evening.

The pool hall was the forbidden part of the building except when you had to go downstairs to the rest room.

Martin Rodosh worked at the confectionery and would have to take ice to the pool hall and sometimes I went with him. The pool hall was just like you see in western movies or those photos of the old west. It had a long bar with a mirror on the wall behind it and lots of glasses stacked on the shelf in front of the mirror. There was a brass rod about a foot off the floor running the full length of the bar. The men standing at the bar would rest one foot on the rod. Brass spittoons were at each end of the bar next to the posts holding up the ceiling. Tobacco chewers would spit in these spittoons. I don't know who had the disgusting job of emptying them. The floor around them was stained brown. The lights were dim. There were several pool tables with a light globe hanging over each one. Tables in the dark corners were for those having a drink and/or playing cards.

I was only twelve years old but that image remains clear. A visit to the pool hall was like a visit to another world for me. I wanted to get back out as quickly as possible When Grant and I slept out on the front porch of our house in the summers we often heard those who had been drinking as they headed for home in lower town. Sometimes we could make out hushed, mumbled words and once in awhile someone would be singing. Very different reactions from men who had been drinking the same kinds of liquor. We lay very quietly until they passed, not wanting to call attention to ourselves and risk an unwanted visit.

In 1944 a new complex of grocery store, confectionery, theater, bowling alley and post office was built in Sunnydale. About this time the amusement hall was turned into a boarding house for single miners. Later the store and mine office were torn down.

The amusement hall was torn down in the fall of 1950. I remember this well. I had gotten home from a Carbon

College baseball game and wanted to borrow dad's truck. He was at the amusement hall with other men and they were tearing up the theater floor. He asked me how the game went, I said we won, and he handed me the keys to the truck with the admonition to "get home early."

Our generation was the last to gather for fun and games at the amusement hall, the town's favorite spot. My grandkids don't have the opportunities to experience the kind of whole-town interaction we had when growing up. Their world is beset with drive-by shootings and the dangers of flashing the wrong hand signals.

In my youth we learned how to get along with each other and have fun thinking up our own games at the old amusement hall. Now movies are in color and shakes are thinner and we could possibly be accused of sexual harassment if we flirted like we did in the old days with Katy Nelson when she worked at the amusement hall confectionery.

This photo taken in the early 1930s shows a bunk house south of the tennis courts. A road has replaced the butcher shop. The house in the center near the creek and railroad bridge was washed away during the flood of 1937. (Photo courtesy June I. McFarland Stevenson.)

THE ASPHALT

With the wife of my youth beside me in our old pickup truck we headed up the canyon to find the tree that I had carved our names in more than forty-five years before. It seemed to me that it was up the right hand fork on the way to the asphalt quarry.

We didn't find the tree but I did find a multitude of memories as I looked up into those mountains. I worked for the asphalt company when I was in high school.

The quarry was located several miles up Sunnyside Canyon nearly nine thousand feet high on the side of a mountain. This is where the oil shale has been deposited over the centuries. The shale is gray. As we walked around the old quarry site, we observed that many of the rocks still have tar oozing from them.

Sporadically from the 1890s to 1948, the shale in this canyon was mined and crushed and used to pave highways throughout the west. My brother Grant and I both worked at the asphalt for a summer or two after we turned sixteen years old. All of the quarry workers rode from the mill at the top of town to the quarry in the back of a stake truck on Monday morning and returned home on Friday afternoon. We took our food for the week with us, and our bedroll the first time up.

On the ride to the quarry there were some steep switchbacks. As the driver would try to shift into a lower gear, at times the truck began to roll backwards. When this happened, all of us riding in the back would be straddling the stake sides of the truck ready to jump if the driver did not find the right gear in time or in case too much stress on the axle would cause it to snap and break. After a nervous half-hour ride we were to the quarry site.

During the week we lived in two men, ten feet by twelve feet wooden cabins that contained a bed, stove, table and two chairs. All the cabins had a dim light hanging from the ceiling, one window and mice. As I recall there were about six or seven of us working at the quarry at a time.

The shale was blasted from the side of the mountain with dynamite, fuses and caps. The large rocks were then loaded into a dump truck and hauled to the top of a large metal tube that led to the crusher. The tube was about six feet in diameter, one hundred feet long, and sloped from the blasting level to the crusher level. A chain at the bottom of the tube stopped the sliding rocks. One man with a pry bar worked the rocks loose one at a time under the chain where they slid to the top of the crusher. It sounded like thunder as the rocks came bouncing and sliding down the tube.

My first job at the quarry was operating the jackhammer. This consisted of holding an air-driven fifty pound, three feet long, vibrating, noisy piece of equipment and operating it in such a way that it broke the big rocks into smaller ones. It had to be done while standing over the crusher. The jaws of the crusher were about fifteen inches wide at the top and about six inches wide at the bottom, which was about three feet from the top. The crusher jaws moved together approximately three hundred times a minute.

My job was to stand with one foot on each side of the crusher with both hands and all of my weight bearing down on the jackhammer until the rock split into crusher size pieces. My main concern was trying to stay out of the crusher when the rock split. The jackhammer had a rope attached to it with the other end of the rope attached to the ceiling so that it could only fall half way into those yard-long jaws if it slipped out of my grasp.

A couple of times my first week on that job, the rope holding the jackhammer picked up an additional 160 pounds as my feet slipped out from under me and I hung on for dear life.

"No problem," I had told the boss when he assigned me to that job. I got it, I believe, because I was larger and greener than my associates. Teenagers do act brain-dead on occasion. I can personally vouch for this.

My associate nearby would work the large rocks under the chain as I was ready for them. Even though my initial response to the boss reflected dead gray matter, I was a quick learner and soon had my associate switching jobs with me from time to time as I rested to gather more strength.

A conveyor belt transported the crushed rock to a large metal bin which had a sliding door on the side. The crushed rock moved about eight to ten miles down the canyon on an aerial tramway. The cable tramway had huge three to five ton buckets spaced about three hundred feet apart. The tram worked by gravity. The loaded buckets going down the canyon would pull the empty buckets back up to the quarry. The tram buckets were unloaded into bins at the "discharge." When the empty bucket arrived back at the quarry, the operator would stop it long enough to pull the rope that opened the bin door to load the bucket again for the trip back down the canyon. It was a unique operation.

At the discharge, about two miles up the canyon from the mill, an operator would slow the buckets as they arrived, disconnecting them from the main cable long enough to move them in front of the four bins where each bucket of rocks was then dumped.

Dump trucks then hauled the coarse crushed rocks about two miles to the mill at the top of town to be processed into asphalt. At the discharge the trucks would pull under a bin and the driver would get out of his truck and pull a rope that released the bin door and the rock would come crashing into the back of his truck. Each bin held enough rock to fill one dump truck.

The trucks had no doors. When we were younger we often hiked up the canyon and the drivers of these trucks would stop and give us rides both up and back in that part of the canyon. Once in the truck it was hang on for dear life. I remember clutching the seat, door frame or dashboard for fear of falling out as the drivers sped along that bumpy, dusty, twisting road.

At the mill the driver would back his truck and unload it into a large v-shaped metal bin with a conveyor belt and catchstrips at the bottom. Here, as another worker tried to stay clear of the rocks being dumped, he would lift up six-inch bars, hinged on one side and covering the belt, and keep the belt loaded with rock which then moved into the mill itself.

The mill contained a series of crushers that continued to reduce the size of the rock until it was suitable to use as paving material. This would then be moved out of the mill on a conveyor belt which dropped it onto a stockpile where it was loaded on trucks or railroad cars and transported to the job site. There was always a large stockpile.

My brother Grant worked at the mill. Just short of two weeks after he graduated from high school, he slipped off a scaffold at the mill and fell, straddling a metal safety rail. In severe pain, he was taken by ambulance to the L.D.S. Hospital in Salt Lake where he was operated on. His injury was serious and it was over two weeks before he was released from the hospital. After two more weeks of recuperation he was given a release to return to work at the mill.

Eight days after Grant was cleared by the doctor to return

to work at the mill, he had another serious accident. His denim pant leg became caught in a cog. The seams in his pants were reinforced and would not tear away. He saw what was happening and braced himself to keep from being pulled into the crusher. Because of the noise of the machinery, his calls for help were not heard and the machinery was not turned off so he could be pulled loose for what seemed to him like an eternity. Before his dilemma was discovered and the machinery turned off, his one pant leg was finally ripped off and two inches on the inseam of the other leg was torn apart. From the force of bracing himself to keep from being pulled into the crusher as the cog continued to pull him, his leg by his boot was seriously bruised. But the worst damage was to his previous injury which now became badly infected. He was taken to the Dragerton Hospital where he remained for two weeks while the doctor worked to clear up the infection. Eighteen days later the doctor signed a release for him to return to work and Grant was once again working ten hour days at the asphalt mill.

My job at the asphalt mill lasted less than two days before I was fired and then rehired and sent to the quarry to work. But, as Paul Harvey would say, "That's the rest of the story."

On my first day at the mill I was to dig away at the asphalt stockpile that had hardened through the winter. My boss saw that it was impossible to budge so said we'd blast it apart. I drilled several holes in the sides of the tall stockpile. The boss gave me several sticks of dynamite, caps and fuses, and five minutes of instructions, including that I was to tamp each stick of dynamite in each hole, make sure no one was nearby and then set the dynamite off.

As a trained blaster, I was now qualified to blow the pile of asphalt apart. I placed the dynamite in the holes and looked for something to use to tamp it in tight. The only tool in sight was the iron crowbar I had been using to pry at the pile, so I began tamping. About that time the boss grabbed me from behind, threw me from my work and uttered an oath I've never heard before or since. As I sorted through his words I learned that by using a metal rod for tamping, sparks could have set off the dynamite and blown the rod through me, or worse. I lost my dynamite qualifications—at the mill anyway..

The boss informed me that the mill would be shut down and we would not be working the next day. I returned to work two days later and the big boss, Ben Argyle, met me in the parking lot and said I was fired for missing a day of work. I related what my boss had said but Ben was not interested. I went home and explained what had happened to dad. He and Ben were good friends. By evening, after dad had a chance to visit with Ben, I was told to return, but that I would be working at the quarry.

When someone asked me why I got fired I replied, "I was fired because of illness. . . The boss got sick of me."

My career with the asphalt company ended when I got a job at the new service station in Sunnydale. On a plaque at the Sunnyside Junction it says, ". . .Asphalt cost $16 a ton to produce and it sold for $8 per ton." This explains clearly why the asphalt business in Sunnyside didn't survive.

As my wife and I finished the trip through memory lane that day at the asphalt quarry site, we saw that there was nothing left but the large rocks, the crushed bin, and the rotted and toppled over tramway towers at the top half of the system. The tramway span over the main canyon, still containing some buckets hanging forlornly above the ground, was still standing, a silent memorial to a once bustling Sunnyside industry.

THE BARN

Last summer my wife and I attended a theatrical production. The newspaper announcement said that it would be held in a barn. As a youngster I had known barn productions; fun and games, but never one with actors—real actors. But then again aren't most kids actors when they are playing out their dreams and fantasies? We surely did that in The Old Sunnyside Barn..

Mention to anyone who lived in Sunnyside during the 1930s and 40s the word "barn" and I can assure you that you will get a reaction and usually a smile. Everyone knew where the company barn was located, who ran it, and what animals it contained. Dad took over the job as barn manager in 1932 after the death of Red Gilligan, who had been the barn manager.

The move to manage the barn meant permanent, steady employment at the mine for dad. In addition to looking after the needs of the mine mules and horses, dad would have steady work at the tipple across the creek from the barn. Our family, consisting of two parents, six children and another on the way, would have to live in the four room house next to the barn. In the move we gave up our upper town status and the one and a half story, with two bedrooms upstairs, house where I was born. But the promise of economic well-being during the Depression was well worth it. The move came soon after my first birthday so I didn't realize that we gave up anything. For me, growing up having access to horses and mules to ride and having a barn to play in was like dying and going to heaven.

My memories of the barn years are vivid, but some of the details are hazy. It seems like the first barn was a small two story wooden building covered with tin. When I was about five or six years old this barn was torn down and replaced with a castle of a barn. I remember the old one being torn down because under the wooden flooring Grant and I discovered old chicken eggs and when we threw them against the corral fence they stank to high heaven. In fact, after the first breeze from the west, the workers tearing down the barn said that if we broke any more rotten eggs we'd have to leave. We stayed, but took the rest of the eggs to the creek bank across the road and threw them against the boulders lining the bottom of the creek.

The new big wooden barn at the foot of the mountain was a real beauty. It had a hay loft much larger than our home. A dirt road cut into the mountain next to the barn made it easy for the hay haulers to unload their bales of hay into the loft. From there we slid the bales to the edge of the openings in the loft floor and fed the animals below by opening the bales and -dropping hay into their mangers.

After the hay was delivered, older brothers Clair and Ned would help us re-stack the bales of hay, making tunnels and small rooms in the middle of the stacks of baled hay. They would also put fear and trembling in our lives by blocking the openings to the tunnels once we smaller kids were inside. Some of us learned after being trapped in those dark, scary tunnels just once. Others, like Ella Ruth, were more gullible and believed their promises not to close off the tunnel ends "this time for sure!"

Two or three hours in the barn playing rubber guns, creeping through the tunnels, or jumping from bale to bale with friends was not uncommon. The hay loft was a great baby sitter. Once we moved into the house by the barn we never lacked for friends. We had the only game in town except for the evening games like Kick the Can and Red

Rover, Red Rover played under the street light in upper town.

In the loft was a large grain bin, larger than any room in our house. A ladder was nailed onto the side which made climbing up to and entrance through a hole near the top easy to access. Another ladder inside the bin made getting down to the grain pile very easy. The grain was funneled to a single opening down on the barn main floor and from here dad and the older boys would fill the buckets of grain to feed the animals.

Mice frequented the grain bin and when a new litter was born, Grant and I were on hand with a shoebox to help raise them. Dad frowned on this activity so it wasn't repeated, but we did enjoy watching those tiny, squirming critters that one time. The grain bin was a fun spot.

The old barn had a harness room but the only thing I remember about it was that it was dusty and dirty. All of the harnesses and leather not in use were covered with dust. The small windows in there were so dirty it was sundown all of the time in that room when the lights were off.

The new barn had a work bench, leather straps and pieces of all sizes, and a riveter. As Grant and I grew older, we made straps, bridles and reins with the leather scraps available. As you entered the main floor of the barn, harnesses and bridles needed for the work animals hung on nails and covered the outside of the harness and leather room. Several horse collars hung among the harnesses. It was a great museum for our young friends.

The harness room even contained tools and templates for putting half-soles on shoes. Dad must have been too busy to get our shoes repaired much because we all remember growing up with 'holey' shoes with cardboard insoles protecting our feet from the rough ground.

The harness and leather room also contained many sizes of horseshoes, nails and equipment for shoeing the horses and mules. Usually shoeing was done by dad and others outside the barn with the animal tied to a nearby light pole. I don't know what had happened by this time to the ornery mules because I don't remember any confrontations between dad and an ornery critter at the new barn.

Since dad managed the barn, we got to keep our own horses there also, once we began acquiring them. When we were not riding them we rented them out to the kids in town at 25¢ per hour. Not a lot of earnings but until we started charging, they rode for nothing. Dad never had any extra money but he understood basic economics.

We even rented out Abe, the big work horse, and Nellie, the gentle mule. Any mount available fetched the 25¢ per hour. When renting and riding with friends we sometimes didn't count the time getting back to the barn. Friends got a better deal so we had a lot of friends.

After World War II, in the late 1940s, electric cars were acquired by the company to pull the cars out of the mine. Thus, the hoist house was eliminated and entrance to the mine was now through Number Two Canyon. Later the coke ovens were no longer needed because of automation at the steel plant in Orem, eliminating all need for mine horses and mules. Thus ended the era of mine animals and our relationship with them and the barn.

During 1947 and 48, mother, Clair, Ella Ruth, Grant and I moved to our Provo home so Clair and Ella Ruth could start their university education and mother could continue to work toward her B.S. degree. When we got back to Sunnyside, the barn and corrals had been torn down and a new barn was built up Number Two Canyon. Things were never the same after that. I was older and wheels had replaced horses in my life, and the walk up the canyon to get the horses was not worth the trouble. Besides, Number Two Canyon could be spooky after dark since there were no lights until you got to the barn, itself.

The memory of the barn and animals will always have a special place in my heart. I believe if more kids today had chores like feeding horses, hauling hay, bringing in wood and coal, etc. there would be less time for gangs, drugs and alcohol. Then again, look at all the channel changing they'd miss.

As we left the remodeled old barn theater that evening I said to my wife that they don't make barns like they used to. And they don't have nearly as much fun in them as we did while growing up in Sunnyside.

Sunnyside's first barn and corral. Most of the horses were eventually replaced by Mules that were needed in the mine.
(Photo courtesy GEA-HBLL-BYU)

BASEBALL

I just read where a baseball player's agent negotiated a $6.4 million a year contract. That's for playing baseball. When I was a boy we did it for fun. Baseball was the payoff for getting our chores done before the sun set. I'd have taken the $6.4 million for the chores and then given half of it back if they'd let me finish the day playing baseball or softball.

We learned the game as youngsters in our backyard in Sunnyside. When you are the child of a coal miner and live in a canyon town and want to play ball, conditions are not ideal. For example, the ball field slopes, ball gloves are in short supply, and you hoped someone had a real bat this time. Our ball field started and ended on a fifty yard slope toward the mountain behind our house. We hit uphill. Hitting uphill decreased the time spent batting because we could never hit the ball hard enough to get it out of someone's reach.

If there were not enough kids for a team, we played "flies and grounders." Catch three flies and you "got up." That was the term used to describe the batter. Nine grounders equaled three flies.

Another way to "get up" and bypass the system was to change the game and play "bat and lay down." This involved retrieving the ball and rolling it back down hill to hit the bat that the batter had laid on the ground after hitting the ball. If the ball hit the bat, bounced up and the batter caught it, you stayed in the field. If the ball bounced on the ground after hitting the bat, you were up to bat.

These games required at least two players who had finished their chores. I envied some of the guys from uptown when they would come to our place to play. Most of them didn't have the same kinds of chores we did so they would either help Grant and me finish our chores or just sit on the porch steps until we were through.

During the 1930s and 40s each town of any size had a baseball team made up of older boys and men. Town teams played each other. At that time Sunnyside's team played on the diamond where the park in Sunnydale would later be located. The diamond was on the northwest corner of the field. There were neither lawns nor trees then, just dust and wind. And no shade anywhere.

Dad had played on town ball teams as a young man and was a great baseball fan. He would take Grant and me in the Chevy stake truck and park so we could watch from the truck or get out and sit on the rise of ground at the southwest end of the field to watch the games. We watched teams from Columbia, Price, Wellington, Helper, Hiawatha, and most of the Carbon County towns compete with the Sunnyside team. I was not much of a baseball fan. I felt the game moved too slow and, when playing, the ball was too hard. On the other hand, softball has been a life-long passion with me.

We had one bad experience in my early years during a family baseball game near Pasture Canyon about a mile above town which reinforced my aversion toward baseball. Grant and I were the youngest so we had to start way out in the field. We were kidding around and joking about playing so deep that we didn't need gloves because the ball would come to a stop before it could get to us. Dad was pitching and big brother Clair was the batter. He hit the ball hard and fast and it traveled straight into dad's face. By the time Grant and I arrived at the mound, dad was on the ground doubled up with pain. Clair had driven his car so he drove dad straight to the doctor. Ella Ruth was too young for a driver's license but she knew enough about driving to drive our truck, with us in it, home.

Meanwhile, the doctor examined dad and confirmed that

he had a broken nose. The gauze pads packed in his nostrils and the tape across his nose made breathing hard for dad for a few days. Eventually his nose healed and it wasn't long before he was rounding us all up for another baseball game. This event may have had something to do with my lukewarm feelings for baseball after that.

During the spring of 1950 I played center field for the Carbon College baseball team. During my growing years I had developed as an average hitter, but I could throw the ball from center field to home plate. My strong arm developed during my earlier years from throwing volleyballs and basketballs in the Sunnyside gym during dodgeball games. Coach Jackson Jewkes liked my accuracy and distance. Sometimes my judgement was lacking, however, as the coach reminded me during one game when we were playing a team from Grand Junction and I ran in at the crack of the bat and the ball went flying over my head.

I gave up baseball after one year even though the new coach, Lyle Kohler, asked me several times to come out and play. I needed the money that an after school job would provide more than I needed the playing time. So I went back to work after school.

With my one year baseball career over, however, I still continued to play softball, my first love, every chance I got. I started playing on church and community softball teams when I was about thirteen years old and I still enjoy the game today. I still play in the Huntsman Senior games in St. George each October.

Town baseball teams continued for awhile after World War II but, with the L.D.S. Church softball programs in each Ward, and the aging of the original team members, the old town baseball teams have found new life in the history books.

When fast pitch softball changed to slow pitch, it gave

new life to some of us middle-aged survivors and the game became much more competitive and enjoyable. Slow pitch softball gives batters the opportunity to learn to hit the ball wherever they want it to go and, thus, lets us old-timers stay competitive with the young hitters.

With modern obscene contracts, lockouts and strikes, baseball has lost some of its greatness as America's pastime. Perhaps sometime it will return to the glory days of o.d. But I wonder if it will ever again mean as much as it once meant to my dad. His love for the game was legendary.

Semi-annual General Conference of the L.D.S. Church is held near the first of October as it has been since the Church was organized. Before the extended baseball season, the Baseball World Series was also held about the same time each year. In Salt Lake City, during my youth, a scoreboard and lighted simulated playing field was placed on the Tribune Building a couple of blocks from Temple Square.

Dad was a devoted Churchgoer and several times in those early years he took his family to Salt Lake City for General Conference. On one trip while attending Conference, he told mother he was going to take Grant and me for a walk since we were getting a little restless. We walked to the Tribune Building and watched a World Series game unfold on that lighted scoreboard. When the announcer would say, "a left field drive!" a string of lights would take us out to left field on the side of that building. I thought that was the greatest thing since sliced bread. At the end of the game we walked back to Temple Square and were near the Tabernacle door for the Conference closing prayer. Mother soon joined us at that door. She had enjoyed the closing hour of Conference in peace as each of us did our favorite thing that afternoon so long ago.

We miss dad and his family activities. But, with the TV channel changer at hand now, baseball seems to move along a little faster than it did in my early days.

THE BATHHOUSE

I don't know that the mining camp bathhouse should be required reading for everyone, but those of us who evolved from the round, galvanized Number 5 bathtub in the kitchen to a shower in the bathhouse will have no trouble relating and retelling our experiences.

Growing up in the vicinity of the Sunnyside bathhouse and watching the miners come and go, created an anticipation in me much like a fourteen-year-old waiting to get his driver's license.

Perhaps it was because I was outgrowing our small round tub. Or perhaps it was the look of that gray water when I was the third or fourth person to recycle the same water over my head and body. Whatever the reason, I was ready to go when older brother Clair asked Grant and me if we wanted to go to the bathhouse with him one Saturday afternoon.

I had thought about going to the bathhouse during my early teen years, but I knew walking toward the bathhouse with a towel hiding clean shorts inside would be a dead give-away. And besides, I'd have to cross the footbridge, walk past the tipple crew, and possibly dad, and go under the tipple and up the steps to the bathhouse. Or, I could have taken a chance and walked across the main bridge, cut across the railroad tracks, run up the hill and past the lamp house. But surely Howard Jones, the friendly lamp man, would begin to ask questions. I guess it was lack of confidence and fear of being turned away that had, until that day, kept me close to home and our round, undersized bathtub.

But that eventful day we got in Clair's car and drove to the bathhouse. What a way to get clean! And we didn't have to empty the used, dirty water. It left on its own power, right down the drain in the floor. We returned there with Clair a few other Saturdays after that.

The bathhouse was a large building about forty by sixty feet. On two opposite sides there were rooms with a long row of showers. In the large main room there were several long rows of benches. Every two or three feet, near the back of the benches, there was a small rope that was looped around a pulley anchored in the ceiling. On the other side of the pulley and the other end of the rope were several hooks.

A miner would come to work in his street clothes and go to the pulley that contained his dirty work clothes. They were hanging from the hooks on that rope up near the ceiling. He would untie the rope and let his work clothes down. After changing into his work clothes, he would attach his street clothes to the hooks and pull them, shoes and all, back up to the ceiling. There they would hang, out of the way, until his shift ended.

The hooks sometimes held a can or basket for his soap, washcloth and towel. Everyone who used the bathhouse knew where his things were hanging. A new employee would have to find an empty rope and that would become his for as long as he worked at the mine.

Some miners, like dad, didn't use the bathhouse much but, instead, returned to their homes to bathe and clean up. Several houses in upper town had bathrooms with tubs or showers. Those who stayed at the "Jap Hotel" bathed in a large, community, canvas bathtub.

After a few trips to the bathhouse under Clair's supervision we, and some of our friends, felt comfortable enough to go about it on our own. We always tried to go between mine work shifts. This way, we figured no one would ask us to leave and we would have the showers to ourselves.

One time, however, we were just finishing our showers

as the shift changed. Talk about an eye opener. When the showers began to get crowded with miners needing to get rid of the coal dust on their faces, arms and hands, it was a sight to behold. Here they were, men of multiple nationalities and every shape and size. Everything about them was black with coal dust except their torsos, teeth and eyes. That sight taught me about an event in history that I could now relate to. When one of the Revolutionary War officers said, "Don't shoot until you see the whites of their eyes," I now understood what he meant. I knew what the whites of their eyes looked like that day in the bathhouse.

Talk about a slurry system. Before that day I didn't know that drain pipes could handle that much water mixed with coal dust and still remain open.

My pals and I got finished as fast as we could and determined that we would use the bathhouse between shifts or not at all. When we had put our clean clothes on the benches, we had taken someone's place. We weren't about to do that again.

Years later when I worked at the tipple, I would come home from college in Price, go to the bathhouse and change into my work clothes. I now had a pulley and hooks of my own. After work, I would shower and change back into the clothes I had worn to school, and go courting.

Living in today's world, as I look back I marvel at how trusting we all were. When I put on my work clothes and left my school clothes hanging near the ceiling, I knew it would be over seven hours before I would see them again. Those school clothes contained my wallet and money, driver's license, watch and any other personal items I had on hand. Nothing was ever touched and I never heard of anyone missing anything from the bathhouse. What amazing trust and respect we had for each other's belongings.

Up until we left home, most of the young men of my day who didn't have inside bathrooms used the bathhouse facilities. Mother and my sisters weren't so lucky. They had to squeeze into the little round bathtub in the kitchen as ong as we lived in Sunnyside.

One prank concerning the bathhouse I remember well was when dad and my cousin Wade decided a new crew member who came to work with them needed to learn a lesson. This new man always showed up just as the shift was starting. He was never early and never did more than he was required to do. He only pulled his share, and barely that. When the whistle blew at the end of the shift, he already had his lunch bucket and was headed for the stairs to the bathhouse so he could be first and not have to wait for a shower.

Dad and Wade got a great idea. They were full of great ideas if a few laughs were part of the outcome. They decided to nail his lunch bucket to the wooden seat in the warming hut, and make sure he was dropping a loaded car when it was time for the whistle to blow.

The new man was headed back up toward the tipple after dropping his car when the whistle blew. He was on a dead run when he grabbed the handle of his lunch bucket. His arm jerked but his momentum kept him moving and he ended up with just a lunch bucket handle in his hand. His bent, twisted lunch bucket was still nailed to the seat. He let out an unprintable oath as the whole crew laughed, whooped and hollered. They all reminded him that others should be first in the shower once in awhile.

He was still cussing up a storm when Wade handed him a new lunch bucket that he and dad had purchased the day before when they plotted this prank. This was just one of the many pranks and practical jokes that took place during dad's tenure at the tipple.

As I visit my kid's new homes with three and a half bathrooms and a hot tub, and listen to them tell about their personal bathroom off the master bedroom, I recall the good old days when my choice was either a bath in the small, round, Number 5 tub or a trip to the company bathhouse for a real shower.

I'd still take the bathhouse convenience, trust and respect of those days but, if I get a choice, "Turn up the jets on that hot tub, thanks!

Mrs. Dimmick's Boarding House

Sunnyside Hotel
Boarding House Lower Town (Photos courtesy GEA-HBLL-BYU)

BORN OF
GOODLY PARENTS: DAD

The Book of Mormon begins with the Prophet Nephi declaring, "I, Nephi, having been born of goodly parents, therefore I was taught somewhat in all the learning of my father. . ." I, too, was born of goodly parents and my father taught me well.

In the history of Sunnyside, when the movers and shakers are mentioned, I would put my father's name near the top of the list. And one of the unique things about dad was that his education ended at the end of the eighth grade.

In his own brief autobiography dad wrote, "I started to work when I was 14 years old for the railroad as a section hand. The work was very hard for me being so young, and I was small for my age. The wages were fifteen cents an hour. We worked ten hours a day and made one dollar and fifty cents, but that seemed a lot of money in those days."

During the 1930s to 1950s, dad served in the Sunnyside L.D.S. Bishopric for twenty-five years and in the Carbon Stake Sunday School Superintendency for four years. During this time he also served on the Sunnyside City Council for sixteen years and was mayor for two years. He was a member of the Sunnyside Welfare Association for thirteen years, four years as president of the Board, and was president, vice president and financial secretary of the United Mine Workers local union. During this time he also served on the Carbon County School Board for thirteen years, two as vice president, and served on the Carbon County Commission for four years. He was truly a public servant.

The minutes of the Sunnyside City Council meetings

suggest a couple of things. One was that he liked short, to the point, meetings. Most of the minutes show him moving for adjournment or seconding the motion. They also show that he was concerned about the needs of all Sunnyside citizens, both in lower and upper town. He made sure the street was paved in lower town, as well as the weeds pulled and culverts dug along the sidewalks for drainage.

He left city government when he was elected to the County Commission. The only election he ever lost was his bid for a second term on this commission. This loss came about because he worked to close all of the taverns in the county that were serving liquor by the drink, in violation of state law. The tavern owners and patrons organized against him in a massive smear campaign, promising free drinks if Commissioner Turner was defeated. Dad lost this election by a small margin, but he was always satisfied that he had done the right thing in his unpopular stand in trying to curb alcoholism and drunk driving.

He took his job as an elected member of the school board seriously. I remember many times when teachers or administrators came and met with him in our front room to discuss their problems. He always worked to find a solution where everyone came out a winner. He worked to make the public schools available to all citizens, especially gyms to fill recreational needs for the kids of the community. Principal Harold Hansen always let us borrow the keys to the school so we could play games in the gym. Supervision was never discussed or required. Teenagers, both boys and girls, could ask for the keys and get them. All that was required was that we put things away when we were through, turn off lights and lock up again. The keys were then returned to Mr. Hansen. In my nine or ten years of weekly gatherings in the gym, sometimes with adults but more often just a group of kids, there was never a problem or a concern expressed from Mr. Hansen or the school board. We appreciated this arrangement.

Twenty-five years is a long time to serve in a bishopric, but dad did it faithfully under two bishops. His one-ton stake truck and his time was involved in nearly all of our camping trips and other M.I.A. activities.

With his service to the community and county, plus his full time job, dad didn't spend much spare time at home. And yet, as a teenager, I remember dad being around enough to see that we had work to keep us busy. And on some of our jobs he worked part of a shift with us, making sure we got it completed right. We also had livestock to care for and cows to milk and milk to deliver. After reviewing his many chores and accomplishments, I'm surprised dad was home as much as he was. He was always around when we needed him most.

Each late summer and early fall, dad would make several trips to Utah County in his stake truck, buying fresh fruit and vegetables from roadside stands to take back to Sunnyside, reselling it to the folks in town. Everyone looked forward to his coming by with fresh produce. I don't know that he made enough to pay for his gas but I do know he figured the time spent was part of his community service.

I remember as a young boy going with dad and helping him sort through things and carrying boxes or baskets into different kitchens in town. When he got to Mrs. Lynn's or Lizzie Jones's, he would always discount the price because he knew that both these widows were having hard times. If a bushel of peaches cost him $1 in Provo, he would tell them they could have it for 75 cents.

Lizzie Jones would always say, "Oh, Mr. Turner, you always get such good deals and we appreciate it."

Often some of his customers would say that they wanted

a bushel of this or that but they couldn't pay until payday. Dad would say, "That's okay. I'll come back on payday. I never remember him going back to collect.

Dad was always a goodwill ambassador for Sunnyside. As youngsters, when we rode to Price with him I was always amazed at the number of people who called him by name. It didn't matter if we were at the auction, the scrap yard, a cafe, a bank or a retail store, everyone knew who he was and would call him by name. He always had a comical comment or joke to share and always asked them about their families. All the time he had a twinkle in his eyes as he visited. He truly liked people.

When he was serving on the school board and it was announced that the government would subsidize school lunches for all school children, I was there when dad discussed this with his friend, Gans Durrant. These two longstanding Roosevelt Democrats couldn't believe what they were hearing. I remember Gans saying, "What will be next if they start this?"

Gans would shake his head in perplexity if he were still around these nearly sixty years later to see just how much the government is involved in all our lives.

When dad was on the county commission, one of his assignments was to approve those who were applying for welfare assistance. He never revealed names but on many occasions he spent time phoning members of the family applying, reminding them it was their responsibility to care for family members in need. To him, public assistance was for the truly needy, not those merely wanting to be on the dole.

One of the Ten Commandments states, "Thou shalt not take the name of the Lord thy God in vain." I think dad probably felt that Moses left out the part that said, "except he

who works with livestock or drives in Price Canyon." Dad
was known to quote scripture forcefully when trying to shoe
an ornery mule or when meeting another vehicle in the ruts
of old Price Canyon.

When dad retired from the corral and livestock, and
when they widened and paved the Price Canyon road, he
lightened up and his language improved markedly. He was
pleasant to be around and didn't get upset easily anymore.
And mother no longer had to ask us to cover our ears.

As a senior citizen, father and grandfather, I appreciate
my father more as the years go by. He wasn't perfect, but
who is? Expressing his love verbally to his children was difficult for dad but we all knew he loved us dearly. After his
death we found a book in which he had written letters to
each of his children. In my letter he wrote, "You certainly
brought joy and happiness and sunshine when you came to
our home. . . we love you with all our hearts and thank God
for you. And I hope and pray that I will ever be worthy of
my fine children." Like Nephi of old, I was born of goodly
parents, one of them named Taylor W. Turner.

BORN OF
GOODLY PARENTS: MOTHER

Volumes could be written about mother. She was sweet and gentle and the best example of 'Christ-like' love I've ever known. I don't remember her ever raising her voice or being angry with me. In our family discussions after her death, each of us children told how we had grown up thinking we were the favorite one. That's the kind of mother we had. She had room in her heart for each one of us to be her favorite.

At the end of World War I times were very hard. The mine only worked one or two days a week so, although mother and dad had Dean and Winifred, when mother was offered a teaching job, she took it and continued to teach until the year Ned was born and teaching longer was out of the question. She still worked every way possible to supplement dad's meager earnings. Mother wrote articles for the Deseret News in Salt Lake and the Sun Advocate in Price. She cleaned the doctor's office and the church, did substitute school teaching whenever possible and was the Sunnyside L.D.S. Ward Clerk which, in those days, paid a small stipend. During these financially hard years Clair, Ella Ruth, Grant and I were born. We all remember the work and scarce money but we remember, too, a mother who read to us, played with us, and supported us and dad in every activity and every experience.

Mother never lost her interest in learning and encouraged her children to reach out and take advantage of every opportunity that came our way. She worked out ways to pay for our music, drama and dancing lessons and was an active

member, including being the president, of the Sunnyside
School Band Parents organization, spearheading drives to
earn money for band uniforms.

All these years mother held onto her dream to build a
home in Provo where we children could attend Brigham
Young University and where, hopefully, she and dad could
live after retirement. So when word came that the mining
company was selling some of the empty houses in Sunnyside
mother wrote to her mother, "We scrimped and saved and
bought two houses and all their spare time Taylor and the
boys work up there tearing the houses down—saving every
board and nail possible. It is slow. We've got to go to Provo
to look at lots and if we could finish tearing down these
houses and get a lot, we'd let Dean and Ned stay in Provo
awhile and dig foundation."

And so, in 1936, the home in Provo mother had been so
anxious to build finally became a reality—a dream come
true. This home housed all of her married children at one
time or another while we attended B.Y.U. or worked in
Provo, as well as her brothers' and sisters' children who
needed a place to live when they came to B.Y.U. Mother
made all of them welcome even though it meant more work
for her trying to find room for them all and helping out with
their living expenses when needed. Mother worked and
arranged for the upstairs to be made into an apartment for her
mother, Grandma Larsen, who was welcomed with open
arms to come there and live out her last years. We all, but
dad who continued to work in Sunnyside and commute to
Provo weekends, lived in our Provo home during the years
1939 to 1941 and again 1946 to 1948.

Mother attended Leadership Week at B.Y.U. every year
that she could, took B.Y.U. classes herself the years we lived
in Provo, and university extension classes every year to com-

plete her B.S. Degree. She went back to full-time teaching after Ned was killed in a car accident in 1941.

During this devastating time, as usual, mother was concerned for those around her. On the night following Ned's funeral mother wrote in her diary, "I tried to do as Ned would want me to—not let anyone be lonesome or left out. So I tried to introduce people, especially lonesome looking ones. Two o'clock came too soon. We were almost alone a few minutes with dear Ned. He was dressed so sweet and looked contented. The funeral was good. I imagined dear Ned stood at the head of the casket, smiling or looking pleased."

Mother received her degree from B.Y.U. in 1954. During all those years mother worked for her degree she taught school full-time, held ward and stake church jobs including President, teacher and counselor in Primary; counselor, secretary and teacher in Relief Society and Mutual; Sunday School Secretary and teacher; and Stake Sunday School Inservice Leader, sometimes holding two or more of these callings at the same time. All the while she took care of her family, brought Bob and Deanna home to live after Pauline died and Dean had to go into the Service, made room for and helped Winifred take care of Dianne and Janet when Michael was stationed overseas, supported dad in all his ventures and was involved in civic and community events and opened her arms and heart to all who needed help.

Even after obtaining her degree, mother took classes whenever possible for the sheer love of learning, a love that never left her. She was a gifted storyteller, creative writer, family historian (snapshots as well as words) and genealogist. Her desire to help her students, as well as her children, expand their horizons continued. Mother always had plays, musical programs and creative projects going in addition to seeing that every child in her classes learned the basics well.

At the end of every school year mother took her students to see the Indian writings above town and then on to the mouth of Pasture Canyon for games, contests and picnics. Her last day of school prognostications delighted her students every year. And former students still say to me, "Your mother was the best teacher in the district."

Mother kept a daily diary from the time I was a little boy. In it she recorded all the events of our lives, what was happening in the world as well as the weather and most of the movies we saw. Once, on his way to bed as Ned said good night to mother while she wrote in her diary, he said, nothing more can happen after you've written in your diary."

She recorded things we said and things we did. We all enjoy re-reading some of our own words to her in years gone by. In March, 1936 she wrote, Paul (5 years old) is always asking questions concerning our Father in Heaven and Jesus like: 'Where does our Father in Heaven live? In the sky or above the sky? Is He all over? Has He a house? How does the Spirit enter the body? Does our Father in Heaven cut a hole in us for it to come in?'"

And again in April that same year she wrote, "Today Paul said, 'We just love the good people and we won't take any notice of bad people, will we?' I thought it good logic."

To demonstrate how exceptional mother was, I'm including here excerpts from a one month period in her diary sixty years ago.

"28 March 1936. Cold. Such a day! Woke up and Grant had a rash. Scarlet Fever is around. I knew it must be. Darla Dean got it 6 days ago. . . Dr & Taylor decided Winifred, Ned, Clair and Taylor could move up into the vacant Teacher's Cottage. There's been all the airing of bedding and carrying everything up and Winifred and the boys cleaning and all.

"29 March 1936. Cold, windy. Ella Ruth, Paul, Grant and I have been quarantined in here today. . . Grant is having Scarlet Fever very light. Paul has a sore throat—doctor says sometimes no rash appears, just sore throat—kept him in bed all day.

"30 March 1936. Slight rain today. The clock is up at the Cottage where Taylor & the children stay—so we guess time. Winifred, Ned and Clair came down to see us tonight and stood at the back door and talked. My, they looked good. I wanted to hug them. They think that house is so quiet.

"1 April 1936. Cold. Winifred, Ned and Clair came down and stood on the back porch. Little souls were lonesome and said they were cold. It is hard for them. Father bless them! Taylor went to Helper today to the Union Day. Brought home candy for us all—Easter things too—but can't have them for 12 days.

"2 April 1936. Cold. Got a fine letter from Dean today about his girl. I must write to him and put the letter out to disinfect until mail time tomorrow. Dean is fine—the Lord bless him.

"13 April 1936. Clear and cold tonight. It is Winifred's birthday. Haven't seen her but Ned came down. Said Genevieve took her up a birthday cake—17 candles. Bernice was here and said Beth went over to see her and wanted to give her some hankies.

"12 April 1936. Warm. Easter! And what a nice one for the children. Easter Bunny brought little chickens pulling carts and Easter eggs. Children were so excited! Winifred went with Genevieve and a bunch Eastering after Sunday School. Taylor took Ned and Clair and some of their boy friends up the canyon in the car this afternoon. I got the work done this morning and took Ella Ruth, Paul and Grant and Darla Dean up on the mountain back of our place this afternoon. Could see both up the canyon and down the country - view was grand. We ate lunch, threw rocks down and had a very good time. Tonight we all went up to Watkins for a few minutes.

"18 April 1936. Clear. Been the most lonesome day I've seen in Sunnyside. The 3 little ones and I stayed here and sat on the porch or walked around all afternoon. From here we could not see one soul. Not a car passed. Everyone gone to Price to the Band Parade. Taylor and Clair came home about 8 p.m. for chores and went back to get the children. They stayed for the Mass Band Concert and dance. It was late when they came. Dean was with them. We were asleep & didn't get to see them. Our quarantine is over but we can't go in public for a week.

"19 April 1936. Rained in the night. The others went to S. School this morning (but Dean). we went up to see him (stayed a little away). We walked down home with us. Oh he is a fine fellow. He is thinking quite a bit of Pauline. I hope all is decided wisely. Just talked to him about an hour when he had to leave with Taylor to catch the bus in Price & go back to Provo. It was so short.

"21 April 1936. Clear. The days are so filled with jobs lately I would forget you, Diary, if Ella Ruth didn't remind me. Today the Utah Fuel co. turned the mine water on for the lawns. Carrie Watkins had a baby girl. Mrs. Watkins (senior) brought Darla Dean and Arlis down here about 7 or 7:30 this morning—they were here all day. Carrie was quite sick.

"22 April 1936. Clear then rain. Carrie Watkins baby girl died at 11 a.m. today—lived 11 hours. I've had her children all day & Darla Dean is sleeping here with Ella Ruth. Carrie is quite sick yet.

"23 April 1936. Clear then rain. Didn't write Thurs. night because as soon as supper was over I ran up to see how Carrie Watkins was getting along. The Dr was in the kitchen and said she was dangerously, critically ill. She was reacting exactly as women did for flu and childbirth in 1918. I said, 'Not a chance then?' He said, 'No.' Bernice was there. I ran home, told Winifred to have daddy come down here and stay. Bernice & I stayed all night—didn't come home till about noon yesterday. Dr slept on the couch there all night and stayed till 11 a.m. Friday. Arlin had gone to Vernal to bury the baby. Phoned for him at 6 p.m. Got home at 12 midnight. Dr said she was going gave stimulants—revived, saw her husband and talked.

"24 April 1936. (cont'd) At 4:15 a.m. Carrie went into a sleep. Dr said to awaken him at slightest change. Bernice left at 6 a.m. At 7 a.m. Carrie's breathing was bad. I woke the Dr. He prepared a hypo, felt her pulse, but I don't believe gave it to her. Mrs. Watkins (mother-in-law) got up. At noon Taylor came (he'd been there every little while) and said for me to go sleep. I came home. Hard to sleep. At 3:30 p.m. I got up. Mrs. Naylor was here to phone Arlin's brothers at Rolapp. Taylor came in just at 10 to 4 p.m. and said she just died—call the Dr. Sister Dennison and I did most of the washing and laying her out. At 6 p.m. James Peacock, John Preston Aunt Bernice and I went to Price to arrange for clothes. Got home at 12. Bernice slept here. Oh this is a sad, sad death.

"25 April 1936. Clear. The family came home today after one month of Scarlet Fever and isolation. How glad I am.

"26 April 1936. Cool-clear. Been trying to prepare a little talk for Carrie Watkins funeral. Oh I hope the Lord blesses me that I may do it all right.

"27 April 1936. Cloudy. 11:30 p.m. All through but putting away the bread and writing up Carrie's funeral for the Deseret News. Had it at 6:30 and talked. My voice was shaky. After, Mr. Hardy, school principal, told me it was the best talk he had ever heard. Winifred heard nice things about it, too. Winifred sang in the choir and Taylor took charge and opened. Our family is fine and the Lord is good."

Mother, Ella Larsen Turner, lived all her life as the Savior taught, "Inasmuch as ye do it unto the least of these, ye do it unto me."

THE BOWLING ALLEY

I read not long ago that in one large city the City Council was banning kids from gathering at the mall. Business people at the mall were complaining that the kids were hurting their businesses. It seems that in spite of our great advances in technology, crime and drug use are growing more rampant in modern society. And while much of the mall problem has been brought on by the actions of the kids themselves in this situation, it's too bad because teenagers need a safe place to gather.

In Sunnyside, "mall" (maul) was what a dog could do to you until help arrived. But we did have safe gathering places and business people liked to see us gather because we did spend most of the little money we had at their establishments. In the early days the amusement hall was our gathering place where we had good times together and spent our few coins.

Then things began to change. The Second World War ended. The mine tunnels which had burrowed around the circumference of Sunnyside were re-directed and now headed straight under our fair town. A new business complex was constructed in Sunnydale. The wrecking crew in old Sunnyside stood waiting for instructions. And when they came, the amusement hall, store, post office, school, mine office, churches, Japanese Boarding House, houses and the barn were relegated to our memories as we fondly viewed pictures in our photo albums. All the old landmarks which had been part of our growing up were now reduced to crumbling foundations and weeds.

But the bright side was that the new gathering complex in Sunnydale had its grand opening. Everyone came to visit, sample and cheer. The complex contained a new post office, a larger, with more varieties, store, a new drug store (confectionery became a word we no longer used), a jewelry store and a service station where cars could be washed, greased and fully serviced. Rain had provided the wash jobs in the past. And, best of all, there was a new four-lane bowling alley. We could now bowl without having to drive to Price.

The new bowling alley manager was Gus Burdis. He must have been a kid once because he understood kids. He also understood economics and he was a master at putting the two together. One of the things that impressed me about Gus was that he knew all of our first names and called us by name every time we walked through the door.

The bowling alley had pool tables we could use. The pool hall in the basement of the old amusement hall had had pool tables but they were off limits to kids because that was where liquor, gambling and dim lights prevailed. But now we could enjoy the freedom of using the pool tables in the new bowling alley.

This new facility also had a fountain and sandwich bar, a jukebox, a pinball machine, and a barber shop where one summer barber, Clayton Anderson, let some of us cut each other's hair and we all ended up with shaved heads. The nicks, grooves, steps and bald spots we gave each other were all right—they were just fifty years too soon. We loved meeting at the bowling alley. Those of us with wheels and a job made the bowling alley our second home.

Gus had a brother, Frank, a great guy who helped us improve our bowling skills. He was later killed in an accident at the tipple and we all mourned his death.

Gus had another brother, George, who gave me my first big tip. He drove to the service station one day when I was working. He had a Chrysler convertible with wood side panels. He wanted to know if anyone would wash it and give it a polish? I would and did. George said he was Gus's wealthy brother from New York. I don't know if he was wealthy or from New York, but he did tip well, and he was Gus's brother. I put a two dollar wax job on his car and he gave me a one dollar tip. He did this several times during the next few months.

The bowling alley had a room for parties and a long hallway with tennis tables we could use by the barber shop. When we arrived at the bowling alley and wanted to dance, Gus let us move the jukebox into the party room. If our group became so big we needed more room, the dancing was allowed to extend out into the hall.

The music included our favorite melodies which had the right beat for us to dance the jitterbug with enthusiasm and pleasure. Some of us who are on our feet fifty years later still do something that resembles jitterbugging, but without the same enthusiasm and pleasure. Eunice Shearer was always popular with the boys and taught many of us to dance. Bill Harris from Columbia was one of the best dancers among us. He was always surrounded by girls. We had some great times and happy gatherings during our teenage dancing years.

When bowling first started there were no automatic pin setters. They came along later. The pin setter in those early days was a boy at the end of the lane who, after the first ball arrived, would place it in the ball return and put the fallen pins in a rack hanging above the lane. After the second ball, he put all the pins in the rack and pushed it back down, releasing the pins. After making sure all the pins were in place, he then waited for the next bowler to roll another ball. I got a job as a pin setter for about two weeks, but found I enjoyed spending my time on the other end of the lane. And, besides, I already had a part time job anyway.

It was not long until bowling leagues were started and many of us teenagers got on adult teams and bowled in competition. I got to be pretty good at it with an average score of

160. Once, in later years, as a Richfield resident I bowled a 267. That was a high point for me. My bowling now comes on that rare holiday occasion when my kids or grandkids are looking for something to do. Bowling has always been a fun game for a family.

I returned to the Sunnydale (now Sunnyside) bowling alley not long ago. What a difference fifty years makes. Buildings are like people, they age. Make-up or paint can't really hide the fact we are growing old no matter how much is applied.

The bowling lanes and snack bar haven't changed much but the party room windows are boarded up and it's used for storage. The barber shop is long gone and the sides of the long hall where we played table tennis have stacks of maintenance, cleaning and other supplies. Video games have replaced the pinball and jukebox machines. The pool tables are still there but they, too, are growing old.

I visited with the girl on duty since I was the only one in the place and I didn't come to spend money, just memories of an earlier time. She answered questions out of sympathy for an old man and told me about the new owner and some of the activities. I told her about the old days. She was patient but, since she's not old enough to have many memories of her own, she listened out of politeness, not real interest. I missed seeing Gus's smiling face and hearing him call out, "Paul, it's nice to see you again!

Gus still comes to the Sunnyside reunions and gatherings of the old crowd and he hasn't changed much. He still calls us by name and has that same twinkle in his eye. Every teenager needs a Gus in his/her life. He didn't replace parents, he just reinforced them.

I hope that if there are bowling alleys in heaven, the price won't have gone up too much. And I hope Gus will be there, and that he will still greet me by my first name.

THE BUS

"The bus is coming!" After "mama" and daddy,' these were the first words a child born in Sunnyside learned. Riding the bus was the way of life for most school students in Carbon County, except for the few who lived in Price.

The bus was our ticket to a high school diploma. Everyone going to the Eleventh or Twelfth grades traveled by bus to Price. Those Carbon College (now CEU) students lucky enough to own cars had their own transportation. The rest rode the bus.

In some cases, the bus was a Carbon County youngster's ticket and link to the outside world. My first memory of a bus ride came when my older brothers and sisters had permission to go to the movie in Columbia if they would take me along. Otherwise they would have to baby-sit me at home. They always made the wise choices and we were off for Columbia on the school bus.

In my youth, school district officials made the bus available for many community activities and trips. Before Sunnyside got its own movie theater the nearest one was in Columbia, six miles away. I was a naive, young addition foisted onto the movie goers so I don't know if there was a charge to ride the bus. I suspect there was a nominal one. With a bus load of happy youngsters and a few adults who took time for a movie, we were off.

During that first bus ride in my young life I developed a life-long sympathy for school bus drivers. Whatever they are paid, it's not enough. This was reinforced when, as brain dead teenagers, a group of us almost caused a bus accident on slick roads. But that story will come later.

After the movie that night I must have slept on the ride home since I don't remember the ride or the movie, but I was hooked on the bus ride as a way to get from point A to point B in the future.

Prior to that first bus ride, our crowded car, and family bonding enroute, was the only change of locations I had experienced. When I said that I developed a healthy sympathy for bus drivers, that did not necessarily include my dad, who was always the driver of our family bus (car). If school bus drivers had used the language that dad used when passing other vehicles on the narrow, rutted curves in Price Canyon, I'm sure ACLU spokespersons would have attended School Board meetings much earlier than they did. When something made my dad angry, he could quote scriptures with the best of them.

I believe I was in the Eighth grade when the new Dragerton School was completed and the old Sunnyside School became history. When that transition took place, bus riding became part of the educational curriculum through junior high as well as high school and beyond for those of us who were residents of Sunnyside. My older brothers and sisters didn't get to experience the bus riding to school scene until they graduated from Tenth grade in our old Sunnyside School. But when that school ceased to exist, my younger brother and I got to start that exhilarating experience at a younger age.

Since our house in Sunnyside was located near the center of town, we could catch the school bus on its way to pick up the kids in upper town, or wait until it returned. We always waited for its return. We may have been dumb but we were not stupid. We could sleep an extra eight minutes if we caught the bus on its return.

One unpleasant event marred my bus riding career. It took place on a winter afternoon about eight miles out of Price on our way home from school. The roads were very slick. I remember that ride forty-seven years ago as though it was yesterday.

It was snowing lightly and the roads were snow packed and icy. The school bus had picked us up about fifteen minutes earlier as school let out and we had started on our twenty-five mile ride home. The bus was full of active, high spirited high school kids. The ride was somewhat less than exciting and the going was slow as the driver shifted down for the trip through Cat Canyon.

Some say I was one of the older boys responsible for starting the trouble, but I believe this was stretching the truth. I'm sure that my mother would never acknowledge me as a troublemaker. In any event, the bus was doing a little slipping and sliding, and as we got to the top of the canyon it was also fish-tailing.

The fish-tailing was fun, so when it began to slow down, a few of them (it may have been us) began leaning and swaying across the bus seats. With our shifting, the fish-tailing increased until the bus was sliding back and forth across both lanes of the highway.

The driver had a difficult time keeping the bus under control. He could drive on slick roads with the best of them but now he, and we, were in trouble. He caught a quick glance in the rearview mirror just as we reached an extended angle in our shifting.

He hit the brakes and uttered an oath much like the ones I had heard my father use under similar circumstances. The bus stopped just short of sliding off the road. The driver called the names of several boys and ordered us off the bus seventeen miles from home. As I look back on that event, discrimination may have been involved since no girls' names were called out, and they were participating in the activity as much as the boys were.

When the bus was a mile up the road the driver reviewed his options and hit his brakes again. We who had been discriminated against observed the brake lights coming on.

We cheered and our goosebumps changed to smiles. As we approached the bus, the driver exercised a new option and ordered us back onto the bus. I've often wondered if the fact that my dad was serving on the School Board at the time had anything to do with the driver's change of options.

We finished the ride in silence. The next day the principal met our bus in the parking lot. We had a serious prayer meeting about conduct on the bus in the future before departing for classes.

As a reminiscing senior citizen, other bus experiences come to mind. While residing in Provo for a couple of years when I was a youth, we enjoyed the city bus service. Upon finishing our Saturday morning chores, my younger brother and I would each get 5¢ from mother. The city bus route brought the bus within one block of our home.

We would board the bus for a nickel each and for the next two hours we would get the deluxe bus tour of Provo and Orem. After the complete round we would depart the bus at the place where we had started, one block from home. The Saturday drivers got so they could call us by name and with a wink reminded us that we were keeping the bus company from making a profit with our long rides.

On another occasion a few years ago, I drove a rental truck to Las Cruces, New Mexico, then took the bus home. The bus made stops at most of the communities in New Mexico, northeastern Arizona and southern Utah, taking forty-five hours to make a fifteen hour trip. I was slowly, but surely, cured of my desire to see the future from a bus window. My 'Passion for Bus Rides' had come full circle.

To those who must use the bus for transportation, enjoy the ride. It ends all too soon, especially the last rides that take place in your memory. And that's not too bad, either.

CHICKENS

The other day I asked my grandkids where chickens come from and they said, "From the supermarket." It was in 8th grade biology class that I first learned that chickens came from eggs. When I was a boy, chickens came from the Montgomery Ward Catalog six weeks after they were ordered.

In Sunnyside we raised a few of all the barnyard animals, chickens included. Dad would thumb through the catalog in late February and ask mother what kind they should order this year. Mother's answer didn't matter since we always got Rhode Island Reds. They were hardy and mean.

As a pre-schooler I became the family mail carrier, taking post cards and letters to the post office a block from our house. If there was mail in Box 346, I would stop by the window and ask Mrs. Jones for it. When the chickens arrived, the chirping from the room where she worked made it apparent and Mrs. Jones would say, "Tell your dad the chickens are here."

The baby chicks arrived in a two feet by two feet cardboard box. It was about six inches high and had a lid. Quarter size holes were in the sides and lid. Wire around the box held the lid tight. Four compartments separated the chicks with about six chicks in each compartment. Some years, if dad had steady work, we'd get two boxes.

We kept the chicks in their box in the house near the stove until the weather was warm enough for them to survive outside. They didn't all make it and we always had fewer chicks to take outside to the coop than had arrived in the boxes. We raised, fed and cared for the chickens, selling eggs and chickens to neighbors and others in town. We kept a few hens through the winter for our own use and then started over with new ones the next spring. We always had a couple of roosters on hand, too, to keep the hens happy. We all remember that those roosters were mean and consistently ready to attack.

We invariably had chicken for Sunday dinner, sometimes two of them. On Saturday mother would select these chickens and the head-lopping would take place. On trips to Price when my younger brother, Grant, and I would move excitedly about the store isles with inquisitive eyes dad would say, "You two act like a chicken with its head cut off." Witnessing a Saturday head-lopping when I was a little older, I knew what my father was talking about as we watched the headless chickens flopping and flapping around.

After the head-lopping, the flopping and flapping, and the chickens hanging upside down from the clothesline poles till all the blood was drained, mother would spread out newspapers on the kitchen table and the cleaning began. The chickens were first dunked in a sink full of boiling water. Then the feather plucking commenced. This continued until all the feathers were gone. Then the denuded chickens were placed back on the newspapers where mother proceeded to clean out their insides. This was a messy job.

When the chickens were cleaned, washed and in the pot on the stove, mother carefully folded the chicken entrails, feathers and feet into the newspapers and, lifting up the stove lid, deposited them in the fire. In those days everything to be disposed of was put: in the stove, in the scrap pile, or thrown over the bank of the creek that ran past our house. No need for trash cans or solid waste pits in early Sunnyside.

The boiled chickens, potatoes and gravy, homemade bread, carrots or peas and milk highlighted our Sunday dinners, with cake or pie for dessert. It didn't get any better than this. Cholesterol-free, low-fat, high-energy foods hadn't been discovered yet. No one counted calories. Stress was not ever a health factor. It was something you put up with without another thought as you tried to survive in those good old days.

One event took place with the chickens that still brings a smile when told at family gatherings. Before indoor plumbing, we had outhouses. Not much explanation is needed except to say that they had cold wooden seats in the winter and an old catalog for toilet paper.

When I was about three or four years old and had just completed my duty at the outhouse, I was returning to our house about seventy-five feet away. About twenty steps into the trip an old, mean rooster about as tall as I was began moving in my direction. He had more than a friendly visit in mind. He had done this before.

Sensing a problem, I began retreating to the outhouse at full speed, yelling at the top of my lungs. My older sister, who had witnessed the event from the back porch, alerted mother. Without missing a beat, mother got her broom and proceeded toward the crowing, cocky rooster that was holding me hostage in the outhouse.

In retelling the story after all these years, listeners say mother would have been a great golfer. She took what has been described in golfing terms as 'a chip shot' at the rooster. As the rooster cleared the clotheslines with wings flapping and feathers sailing in all directions, the crowing changed to panic-stricken screeches. I was taken to the safety of the house under mother's protection. We had that tough old rooster for dinner the very next Sunday. If mother were still around I believe she could solve today's crime problems.

Years later a friend and I acquired thirty-five hens one summer. We got a few eggs over the next couple of months and planned to have ready-to-cook chickens in our freezers for the winter. When the time to put our plans into action came I had, unfortunately, just put up a new white picket fence in our backyard. I held the chickens as my partner did the head-lopping. They were then turned loose to do their flapping and flopping. When the neighbors heard the commotion they leaned over the fence to see it first hand.

One said it looked like a battlefield with the body parts and blood on the white fence. Another said it looked like "The Little Big Horn—South." Some chickens made it to the road in front of our house causing more unfavorable comments.

This was my last effort at chicken raising. I'm with my grandkids now. We get chickens at the supermarket.

Chickens were our constant back yard companions while growing up. Here dad helps us with the feeding. (L) Friend Marilyn Brown, Ella Ruth, dad, Paul and Grant. (Photo author's collection.)

CHORES

We were out riding the other afternoon and we stopped by one of our kid's homes just as they were finishing dinner (I never did find out where supper went, but THAT was the evening meal when I was young). The parents were asking their kids to do some chores as the day wound down.

Their dad asked one of the kids to put the dishes in the dishwasher. When I was a boy no one ASKED anyone to do the dishes. If it was your week for dishes, you were pulling them out from under people's mouths before they were through eating. When the meal was finished, the dishes HAD to be done before you could go out and play. Dishwashers? Our dishwashers were those things dangling just beyond our wrists.

He asked another child to wheel the garbage container out to the curb, since the next day was garbage pickup day. Curb? Garbage pickup? Times have surely changed. In old Sunnyside there were only about three homes in upper town with curbs and that was merely where the sidewalk met the asphalt road. What chunks of sidewalk there were rose about four inches above the road. The -cement sidewalks had run from the top of town to the end of lower town at one time, but that was long gone. There were cracked and broken slabs of sidewalk left all through town but there were never enough smooth ones in a row to easily roller skate on. As far as the word 'curb,' if you wanted to use that word in a sentence it would be, "Eating is what you do if you want to curb your appetite."

And what about someone else picking up the garbage? If the garbage went anywhere, you took it. Most of the garbage went to the pigs, the woodpile, the scrap iron pile, or over the creek bank. When we picked up garbage it was to build something out of it. It was re-usable, not garbage. We made scooters, rafts, go-carts, huts and dozens of other things out of 'garbage.'

Their mother then said, "Pop that bag of popcorn into the microwave, please, so we can snack while watching TV." Can you believe that? Popcorn, pre-buttered and in a bag that swells up as the corn is popped! And a device (microwave) that conducts heat in all the directions to bake potatoes or cook dinner or pop corn in a few minutes! And a timer that tells you when it is ready to eat, scant minutes later!

When I grew up, popcorn was a once in awhile deal. It cost money needed for other things most of the time. And when we could afford it, we had to get a handful of corn kernels out of the cloth bag it was stored in on the bottom shelf, put it in a wire cage with a long wire handle and shake it over the stove until most of the kernels had popped. We did eventually see the electric popcorn popper come along, making popcorn much better tasting.

As we were leaving, my son checked to make sure the thermostat was at 70 degrees, even though it was 89 degrees outside. With their heat exchanger/air conditioner combination unit, the room temperature never changes. In the early days temperatures changed with the seasons. We had colds all winter and were sweaty all summer.

Coal and wood were two daily chores that never got left undone, regardless of the season. If they weren't brought in, there was no way to cook the meals or have hot water and, in the winter without these chores done, you could wake up frozen to death. In the summer you didn't open a window for a little breeze making it easier to go to sleep since most of the windows had long ago been painted shut. There were no screens on them anyway and we weren't dumb enough to add flies, mosquitoes and other flying insects to our too hot sleeping conditions. And thermopane glass? When the wind blew in Sunnyside, and it did all the time, it went right through the glass, frames and floorboards.

The outhouse was another thing that nobody missed when it passed into history. Now days there are color coordinated towels and bathroom tissue. In those days old catalogs were our color-coordinated tissues and we were lucky to have that. One of our chores was taking the slop bucket out to the outhouse as often as was needed. We could get into a lot of stories about this chore, but let's not spoil a good story with details.

On baking day, mother used to bake sixteen loaves of bread, starting from scratch—and that included making her own leavening. Now days my wife has about that many in the freezer which she just picked up from the supermarket in case company shows up. And it's all sliced and ready to thaw and eat. But I have to be honest. It doesn't smell or taste nearly as good as that good old whole wheat bread we cut thick and piled high with homemade butter!

Soup was another meal that chores figured in on. There was peeling the spuds, carrots, onions, etc. No one cries anymore from peeling onions like we used to do. For soup we just shake some dehydrated pieces out of the can. And if we want a slice of onion on our barbecued hamburger, we peel and slice ONE, without many tears. But then we used to peel and dice eight or ten at one sitting. And believe me, that will bring tears to everyone's eyes.

They don't wax floors like we used to do, either. My wife has one of those fancy wax-mops that was advertised on TV for $19.95. It almost does the kitchen floor by itself, at least it seems that way when we compare how we did it in the early days. The slabs of paraffin wax had to be melted carefully in a can on the stove then applied to the floor with a rag quickly before it hardened again. We scorched our fingers many times with that hot wax.

And vacuums? Who needed them? Very few people had 9x12 carpets on their living room floors and when those carpets needed cleaning they were hung over the clothesline and hit with a carpet beater until the dirt and dust were gone. Carpeting, as we know it today, first appeared on the back seat floor of the old Hudson cars. From that humble beginning carpeting made its way into our homes. Even into kitchens and bathrooms today.

Ironing? Talk about a boring chore. Little kids did handkerchiefs, dishtowels and pillowcases. About the time we graduated to shirts, blouses, skirts, slips, curtains, table cloths and everything else made of cloth, the boys were tagged for outside chores and the women and girls spent hours dampening, starching and ironing. Now if it isn't wash and wear, it doesn't sell.

And what about fast food? The only fast food we ever had when I was growing up was when a dog chased me home from the store. Even though my freezer is now filled to the top, some of my kids and grandkids still have to have fresh pizza and 7-Up. And french fries. And tacos. And chicken nuggets. In the early days we would have only used that term if the gizzard sack had broken open while mother was cleaning a chicken on the paper-covered kitchen table on Saturday afternoon.

We still shake the throw rugs at our house, but it doesn't stir up the cloud of dust that it did at our old Sunnyside house. 'Course we don't track in the dirt and mud like we used to do then, either. Grass, cement walks and driveways and curb to curb blacktop have cut that rug shaking down by 50%. You can cut it down 100% by running the vacuum over them.

On top of the usual chores, we had other duties. The older boys fed the livestock and milked the cows. The younger ones gathered eggs, fed the chickens and delivered milk and eggs. The girls helped with the egg gathering sometimes but their other duties included helping wash and stretch curtains, wash windows, do the washing with the old fashioned wringer washer and hang all the clothes to dry on the clotheslines, winter or summer. Then gather them in (stiff as a board in the winter), fold and dampen them to be ready for ironing.

Most of our regular chores were assigned by the week and they rotated each week. On Saturday, mother made a list of the things that we had to do before we could go play. The list was divided into smaller lists, depending on the number of kids who were still living at home. The person dividing the lists was last to choose his or her list. These lists were always made as fair as possible since the list-divider got the last list left. We didn't have to be reminded to get with it. The sooner you got your chores done, the sooner you got to go play.

Because we had horses, a big barn to play in, and most of the team and equipment for a softball game, plus some old cars to work on and ride in, our place in the center of town was quite popular. Kids living in upper or lower town showed up at our place every day. Often several boys and girls would be waiting in our yard or on the back steps as we worked to finish our chores. Once in awhile they pitched in to help us finish early. Then it was off for fun and games. In the early evening it was back home again for the evening milking, feeding, etc. plus haircuts and baths. This was a typical Saturday.

The chores and other duties taught us responsibility and dependability. Nearly all the kids in town were learning the same work habits we did. Most parents today are struggling to instill this same sense of responsibility in their children but, with today's modern conveniences, it's harder to teach kids the things that we learned naturally in order to survive.

Although most of us do not want to go back to the good old days, it would be nice if we could teach all of today's kids the values and family togetherness that we enjoyed in our growing years.

As my son leaves for his second job and his kids depart for dancing class, little league, and part-time jobs, I can't help thinking how easy it was to raise kids in the early days. Just give them enough chores and responsibilities and don't worry about where the money will come from to hire extra cops . . . they won't be needed.

CHRISTMAS

I'm not as crazy about Christmas as I was when I was a kid. Two things are responsible: I learned the real Santa story, and my wife's shopping habits.

My wife does Christmas shopping every day but Christmas and Sundays. If I'd have known that she would never stop buying gifts for nine children, many in-laws, and thirty some grandkids, I'm not sure our hand holding in the early days would have progressed much further. She buys a lot of gifts, starting December 26th and ending December 24th every year. She never misses sending a birthday gift either. Talk about your weeping credit card.

I don't pay off her credit card each month. A maxed out card is a good reminder not to use it. If the machine does not approve her card, she just says "charge it." What merchant would turn her down? Five merchants in our town remain in business because of her.

Each year before the Fed decides on interest rate changes they call my wife and see what spending she'll be doing. If the grandkids keep coming, this spending could get out of hand. Now, years ago in Sunnyside . . .

We went to the canyons and cut our own Christmas trees. The decorations included last year's icicles, one string of colored lights, a few glass ornaments and the star on top. In school we made green and red chains out of strips of construction paper and also threaded popped popcorn on a long string. On good years we had a tinsel rope draped around the tree.

There was a red wreath with an electric candle in the center to hang in the window. When the cord became brittle and bare wires showed, we still hung it in the window. We just didn't plug it in anymore.

In those bygone days there seemed to be more snow in Sunnyside than anywhere else. Maybe it was because I was small and six inches of snow covered my boots, or maybe it had to do with the ozone layer and glacial warming. Or it may be that in our canyon town that great snow shovel in the sky had a shorter shining time. Who knows?

There were no lots where you could go and buy a tree. The closest thing to that was the years we cut extra trees, hauled them off the mountain and sold them from our front porch for fifty cents each. Grant and I did this for three or four years. When the good trees near the roads were gone and we had to hike higher and higher through deeper and deeper snow, we had to raise our price. After one grueling trip for trees, when one woman said she would never pay one dollar for a tree, that was the year we gave up this enterprise. It was only a few years later this same woman had to pay many times more than she said she'd never pay to get a tree.

There were no outdoor decorations. One very special man in Sunnyside, Bones Watkins, lived in the apartment above the hospital and he began decorating and lighting a tree and placing it on the first floor roof for everyone in town to enjoy. It enhanced the Christmas season and added great pleasure to youngsters sledding in upper town.

My older siblings tell me Jimmy Lynn played Santa when they were young but for as long as I can remember it was Buster Preston who put on his Santa suit and became the jolly old man himself as he attended church, school and other Christmas parties. He also visited every house in town on Christmas Eve. The Union would provide him with small sacks of candy and nuts for every child in town.

The first thing I remember about this life is standing in my crib crying when Santa showed up at our house on Christmas Eve. The bed was in the front room near the stove and front door. My older brothers and sisters calmed me down long enough to get my sack of candy. From then on, Santa and candy were special favorites.

We were living and going to school in Provo when I was in the third grade. That Christmas, teachers Mrs. Leichty and Mrs. Ellsworth, did their best to keep the Santa story going, but my pal Ralph Olsen had given me the straight scoop about that jolly old fellow and my Christmases after that were never the same.

Back in Sunnyside, Christmas was a great holiday, especially during my adolescent years. Once Bones started his outdoor Christmas tree, the town leaders picked up on it and got a giant tree for the lawn in front of the amusement hall every year. This tree had strings of large colored lights and was large enough to hide in during our games of tag. In our free time, most of us kids in town hung around the amusement hall to visit, play games and just have a good time together.

Back in those early days one great gift our family got from Santa was a large Flexible Flyer sled that could hold four or five yelling, active kids as it slid along the icy street of upper town from in front of the hospital down to Lizzy Jones's house. Four of us would sit jammed together on the sled with the front guy steering with his feet. The fifth person ran behind pushing on the back of the last rider. When full speed was attained, about as fast as a guy with bulky galoshes on his feet could run, the guy pushing jumped on for the ride. Often there was not enough room left on the sled so he would just jump on the heads and shoulders of the four seated riders.

One of our greatest disappointments was the year we got back from a summer in Provo and found that great sled gone from our cellar, where it had been stored every summer. We never did see it again but hoped whoever took it had as much fun on it as we did.

Every Christmas Eve everybody in town gathered at the schoolhouse gym for the Christmas Dance. Homemade root beer, bubbling with dry ice, and homemade ice cream topped out a fine evening. Then it was home where, when you were small it was right to bed and, when you became a teenager, you got to help fill the stockings with goodies and sometimes help Santa.

The old Sunnyside Christmas season was a great time for dances and parties. Sometimes the parties were at our house and sometimes they were at friends' houses but they always included food with all the trimmings: homemade ice cream and root beer, sandwiches, pies, cakes, cookies and candy. We also had lots of homemade eggnog. The thought of drinking all those raw eggs turns my stomach now but, in those days, eggs, milk, sugar and cinnamon made some wonderful drinks.

The Christmas season was a great time for youngsters to go ice skating, sledding, skiing, tobogganing or bizzing (hanging on to a car's back bumper and sliding on your shoes), or just plain, good, old-fashioned snowball fights.

All the drivers in town got their cars or trucks stuck in the snow often, but there was always some help nearby to push them out. I don't remember many snowplows. We just packed the snow on the road until it turned to ice and joined the fun. Milk deliveries on our bikes were a little more difficult, and the corrals were more soggy and smelly but, overall, Christmas in Sunnyside was one of my favorite holidays. And with school out for at least a week, we made it fun full time.

I wish I could take my grandkids back with me to the Sunnyside of the 1930s and 40s. They would learn how to have more fun with less, and just how much fun group activities can be. It would also be a great lesson for their parents to see how we spent a lot of time giving to those who had nothing and made sure the gifts were what kids really needed. When I was a boy we got one or, occasionally, two gifts from Santa. I've seen kids today throw away more gifts on Christmas night than we used to get Christmas morning. Joy and fun are created in the mind, not in the accumulation of material things. All of us today need these reminders.

In the fifty years since those days in Sunnyside, the snow depths have changed along with the number and variety of gifts available. But I believe I'd still take my new gloves and Flexible Flyer sled over today's Nintendo, Power Rangers or Barbies. Or would I? That Nintendo can be a fun game on a cold winter day and one of these days I'm going to win.

Sunnyside's first Hospital was located in Hospital Canyon, behind the school. (Photo courtesy GEA-HBLL-BYU)

Later a new Hospital was built across the street from the School House. (Photo courtesy Ernie Romero)

The Hospital and School House. It appears the doctor and his family posed for a family photo. (Photo courtesy Renae Swenson Blackburn)

CHURCH

The two things I remember enjoying most about church in Sunnyside were the closing prayer after a meeting, and rolling down Pressett's lawn. Their house was across the road from the church and on a hillside. Their front lawn sloped down toward the church.

No. It goes much deeper than that, especially in today's world where values are no longer well-defined, and language and morals seem to be reaching their lowest common denominators. The church and a good family provided me with the basics which are a great influence in my decision making processes today. For this I'll ever be grateful.

Our L.D.S. Church building was about thirty feet wide by sixty feet long. The outside wooden walls were painted gray and the steep roof consisted of weathered shingles. Originally there was a steepled bell tower above the front doors, but this was gone before I was born.

Inside there was the large meeting room and a ten feet by thirty feet stage at the west end. Halfway up the back wall on this stage was the only electrical outlet, aside from the ceiling light fixtures, in the building. The socket was often empty and some of us learned about 'shocks' by sticking our fingers in this socket. We were dumb, but lucky that the electric power was very weak in that line. Behind this stage was the fifteen feet by thirty feet Relief Society room. A basement under this room provided for two small classrooms. These rooms were not used during the winter as they were impossible to heat.

A furnace cellar underneath the south side of the building contained the coal furnace and boiler that provided radiator steam heat, if someone remembered to fire up the furnace well before meeting time. Several times, after our family was no longer responsible for this job, they didn't.

Long narrow windows graced the walls on either side of the meeting room and in the winter it would have been better if we could have met closer to the high ceiling where it was somewhat warmer. The clapboard and plaster walls and plank floor were all uninsulated.

A small pump organ was located near the stage on the southwest side of the meeting room. We call it 'chapel' now but in that old building there was only the one large room for all kinds of gatherings. The organ took foot power to operate, but it rang out loud and clear and carried a melody better than some in the congregation did. The organ had a row of pull-out knobs that added different tones. The stool for the organist was a round seat on a pedestal with a three-clawfeet base and the seat could twist right off the pedestal with enough turns. Ella Ruth was the Sunday School organist during most of her junior and senior high school years.

Our family did the church janitorial duties for several years when I was growing up. This work included a very small stipend. Ned and Clair stoked the furnace and took out the ashes in the winter. We all swept the floors and cleaned and dusted the place every Saturday. Dad served in the Bishopric for twenty-five years and, besides being in the Relief Society and Primary Presidencies, mother was the Ward Clerk for a few years. In those days the Ward Clerk received a very small salary.

The seats for the congregation to sit on were wooden, folding four-seat benches. We folded them and leaned them against the walls prior to sweeping the floors. After sweeping we would arrange them back into rows. Sometimes we just slid them back, sweeping one row at a time, then moved them back into place. There were a few single straight-back wooden chairs near the door for late arrivers. The stage and classrooms contained an adequate number of folding benches and single chairs.

The entrance to the building was from the east side, opposite the stage. There was a back door from the Relief Society room with long wooden steps leading to the ground, but that was only used in emergencies. I don't ever remember going out that door.

Sunday School classes were divided by age groups with classes meeting in the corners of the main room and on the stage. Teachers had to speak in soft tones or the voices quickly became stereophonic in that big, echoing room. The basement classrooms were separated by a door so, during the summers, more lively discussions took place there. Obviously, these were the best rooms in which to teach rambunctious teenagers.

We all learned how to give talks while moving through the Primary and M.I.A. programs, and with 2½ Minute Talk assignments in Sunday School. There were no microphones so we learned to speak clearly and loud enough to be heard throughout the room. The speakers and those giving the prayers sat on the stage along with the Bishopric and Ward Clerk.

The baptismal font was located under a trapdoor on the stage floor. This font was about four feet wide by eight feet long and looked very deep the first time that I saw it. I was baptized by dad in that font soon after my eighth birthday. The tap to fill the font carried cold water only. For winter baptisms, five gallon milk cans of hot water were carried from nearby homes and emptied into the font to take the sting off the cold water but this never really warmed the water much. At a recent Sunnyside Reunion Ivan and Ned McCourt told about their baptisms in that cold, old fort.

The McCourt family was living in the house just north of the church at the time. It was January and the water in the font was ice cold. Ivan said that dad, who was going to baptize him, and others brought buckets of hot water to take the chill off the water in the font but by baptism time it was cold again. Their dad was not a member of the L.D.S. Church but had given his approval for them to be baptized. Ivan was eleven years old at the time and Ned was eight. Ivan was the first of the two to be baptized.

Ned now picks up the story, When I saw Ivan turning blue with the cold water and covered with goosebumps, I decided that this was not the time for me. I was dressed in a white shirt and pants, but no shoes. I ran from the church through the snow back to our house barefoot." Then he added, "I did get baptized three years later . . . in the summertime."

Ivan finished the story by saying that after he was baptized he ran, wringing wet and with no shoes, to his house next door. Both of them had high praise for dad, Bishop Hopkins, Jim Peacock and others who took an interest in them as youngsters.

Several meetings were held at the church each week. The M.I.A. young people's organization met each Tuesday night. If an activity was involved we'd meet at the church for Opening Exercises, attend the activity (sledding, service projects, games at the school gym, etc.) and regroup at the church for the Closing Exercises. Primary, the organization for children, was held every Tuesday for an hour after school. Sunday School was held Sunday mornings and Sacrament Meeting was held every Sunday evening. Priesthood Meeting was usually held before Sunday School and Relief Society was held once a week during the week. In order to save extra firing up the furnace in the winter, Relief

Society was usually held Tuesday during school hours.

Although the room behind the stage was designated the Relief Society room, it was used most of the time for storage. Most Relief Society meetings and activities were held in the main room. The Relief Society sisters made many quilts, both quilted and tied. When Grant and I attended Relief Society with mother, we would take our places under the quilt to be tied. When mother and some of the other ladies would push the long needle threaded with yarn down from the top of the quilt, we would push the needle back up through to them. There was no Nursery in those days and for active youngsters it was a make-work project. And it worked. It kept us out of mischief. The quilts were usually heavy but still not warm enough individually to stave off the cold winter weather in Sunnyside. Every family needed plenty of quilts.

Clair taught me how to ride a bike while we were at the church. One Saturday when we were cleaning we went outside and I leaned Clair's bike against the fence and climbed on. He gave me a push, yelled, "Pump!" and I was off I didn't know how to stop it or get off, so at the tennis court one block away I turned the bike uphill and quit peddling. The bike stopped and I fell off. I pushed the bike back up to the church and tried it again. For the next few days Clair taught me all the other skills necessary to become a bike rider.

For dances, wedding receptions, quilting bees, ward or M.I.A. games and activities, the benches in the main room were pushed to the walls and out of the way. We had some great times in that good old building.

With dad in the Bishopric he was able to watch us wiggly little kids from the stand and, with a long, stern look, nearly always get us to settle down. Since I was near the end of our family tree there was no one for me to tend during church, but my older brothers and sisters weren't so lucky. And, yet, I don't remember any of us ever being carried outside to be disciplined.

All the modern L.D.S. Church buildings have large parking lots, recreation halls, libraries, rest rooms, many classrooms, baptismal fonts with warm water, microphones and an organ in the chapel and pianos in the chapel, Relief Society room and Junior Sunday School room, but I wonder if they can create the memories that our old Sunnyside church did.

LDS Church group (Photo author's collection)

CLOTHING

As our youngest was preparing to leave for college my wife informed me that she was removing my things from "her" closet. She had been threatening to do this for years. It didn't matter that she had clothes in three closets. My clothes took up only three feet of rod space. I was getting kicked out. I had lost my closet rights.

My wife does not get rid of clothes. Her wedding dress and Junior Prom formal still hang in the closet. When asked about them, she says that we may need them sometime. Never mind that her wedding dress is turning brown with age and the prom formal would not fit again even if a slim down diet worked.

I'm moving my twelve hangers of clothes. I'll put them in my son's closet as soon as he takes his to school with him.

It wasn't like this in the early days in Sunnyside. Let me share an entry from mother's diary. My wife enjoys the diary, but does not like me to keep reading this entry to her. It says, "Today we went shopping in Price. I got two new dresses. They are the first new ones I've had in ten years. They cost $2.00 each. How happy I am."

If two dresses in ten years made my mother happy, my wife should be hilarious all of the time. Hanging my clothes in my boys closet will be temporary at best. Some day I'm sure we'll arrange for a small self-storage unit as their final resting place.

Not only did my mother not have many dresses but, compared to today's standards, we were all underdressed. We did not discard old clothing. We recycled it over and over again. The bigger kids clothes were taken apart and sewed back together until the seams would no longer hold. Then they were cut down to fit the younger kids. Ella Ruth remembers she was thirteen years old when she got her first new store-bought dress, made of beautiful rust colored taffeta. When the clothes could no longer be worn, they ended their days as rugs. More about that later.

As a youngster of the 1930s, I owned two pair of overalls—one for school and one with patches for all the other times. I also had a Sunday pair of wool trousers and a long-sleeved cotton shirt, both of which mother had made out of some my older brothers had outgrown.

When our underwear and socks became ragged, they were recycled. Mother patched and mended them on her treadmill, powerless sewing machine. Even the cloth sacks the flour came in was recycled into dish towels or 'bloomers' for the girls. When underwear and dish towels finally became completely worn out and mother was satisfied they had served their purpose, they became rags and then rugs. When the fabric's wear was doomed, it advanced to its final resting place; on the floor as a new rag rug.

Here's how it worked: Mother would put all the clean, worn fabric items in a gunnysack in the closet. All family members would be involved in cutting the cloth into one inch wide strips, putting these strips together into another bag near her sewing machine. Mother would then sew the strips together, end to end, making a long, one inch wide cloth rope.

We kids would then wind the long continuous strip into a ball of cloth. The round balls of cloth would grow to the size of a volleyball or larger. The balls would then be placed into another gunnysack to wait for their trip to a weaver in Price who would turn them into new rugs.

When we cut a sock into a one inch strip, we cut it in a circular motion, trying to make it just one long strip. Dad always peeled apples the same way, one long continuous strip of peel.

Three months after taking the sacks of cloth balls to Price, the new throw rugs arrived back home after one of dad's trips for feed. These two and a half feet by five feet rag rugs would be placed in the heaviest traffic areas of our house, with the old ones moved near the doors to wipe our feet on before coming inside. The rugs became part of our family.

As we unrolled each rug, laughing and pointing, we would identify our former clothing by its colors in each rug. If one had enough of your former clothes in it, it became your favorite rug. When footprints had taken their toll and the rugs were worn out, the remains became part of the fuel for our coal stoves. The recycling, along with some nostalgia, became complete.

One clothing story I remember well was when our brother, Ned, was killed in an automobile accident. His well-worn suit hung in the closet until I was big enough to wear it. The pockets were worn out and the suit had some shiny spots, but it was a reminder of a brother we all loved and missed. When I outgrew that suit I'm sure that it did not become part of a rug. Knowing mother, and her sorrow in losing a child, I'd like to think that she would dispose of it like she would a worn out flag, placing it in the fire in a quiet ceremony when no one was watching. Mother was like that.

The next suit I owned was when I got married and it was not a hand-me-down. I still have fond memories of that suit.

As I begin transferring my clothing from my old closet to their new temporary quarters, I long for the old rug weaving days. Not only would it keep today's kids busy, but I've identified some of my wife's clothing that would make colorful rugs when she isn't looking. Then again, perhaps the divorce rate would become even higher if husbands began recycling their wives' clothing. It's something to think about.

THE COKE OVENS

Several years ago, after some of my sons and I had just spent a long day loading and unloading one of our moving vans, one of them remarked that they didn't know of anyone who worked harder than us. I said, "Those are the very words I told my dad years ago when I DID work at the hardest job in the world."

I was fifteen years old when my brother Grant, a year younger, and I approached dad, reminding him that we had to be sixteen to work at the asphalt company and we were not making enough money at paper routes and delivering milk. Could he help us find higher paying jobs? Dad could, and did.

Dad knew the scriptures: "In the sweat of thy face . . ." Gen. 3:19; "Six days thou shalt labor . . ." Deut. 5:13; ". . knowing that tribulation worketh patience . . ." Rom. 5:3; ". . . cast them into the burning fiery furnace." Dan. 3:20. And, of course, several references to "long suffering." With a twinkle in his eyes he said that we were to go to work the next morning at the Coke Ovens.

About the turn of the century coal was discovered in Whitmore Canyon, twenty-five miles east of Price. The coal was much better for coking than that mined at Castle Gate. In the early part of 1902 the building of coke ovens in Sunnyside commenced. They continued being constructed until when World War I began there were 819 beehive type ovens built. By 1918, when all the ovens were in operation, it took about 2500 tons of coal per day to keep the ovens running seven days a week.

During the late 1920s the demand for coal and coke was greatly reduced. The coke ovens operation shut down in

1927 and stayed shut through the Depression. In the late 1930s the onset of World War II in Europe caused the coal mining operations to increase and the coke ovens to resume operation again as part of the approaching war effort.

The ovens were connected on the outside with a straight brick wall which ran in several long rows. The inside of each oven was shaped like a ten feet across, ten feet high beehive. On the top of the ovens and outside walls was where the train cars traveled and unloaded eight tons of coal into the small, round opening at the top of each oven. At the front of each oven was an opening about the size of two kitchen cabinet doors. These were bricked up for the coal inside to be burned and taken down when the coke was ready. A road about ten feet wide in front of the ovens extended the full length of the walls of ovens.

Opposite the ovens was a ten feet high rock wall with the upper edge the same level as the road. At the bottom of these walls were the railroad tracks and empty railroad cars which extended about three feet above the rock wall. The coke was "pulled" from the oven into a pile below the oven door. From there it was shoveled into a wheelbarrow. The wheelbarrow was then pushed up a one foot by twelve foot wooden plank, with the operator emptying the wheelbarrow into the railroad car while balancing on the plank.

Eight tons of coal was loaded into each oven and in three days the flames and heat had turned it into five tons of coke. As the openings were re-bricked and the oven loaded again, the coal caught fire immediately from the intense heat still in the oven.

Dad had told us to get to bed early. He was right. At 4:30 a.m. his fingers tapped on my forehead, signaling me to get up. By 5:15 dad, Grant and I were at the coke ovens a mile below town. The foreman met us and smiled as he showed us what each piece of equipment would be used for. Dad already knew but listened for the next fifteen minutes with us, a hint of a knowing smile twitching his lips occasionally.

The oven we were going to "Pull" was at least a million degrees in temperature as we pulled the bricks from the opening.

A horizontal rod and pulley were located in the middle of the opening. This pulley permitted the oven tools to move in and out of the oven. With the bricks removed from the opening we "cooled' the coke by spraying it with water. This was done with the use w of a twelve feet long pipe with a spray nozzle going into the oven. The handle end was hooked to a water hose and stand pipe. With the water turned on, the steam pouring out the oven top and opening was very intense. After ten minutes the oven was considered "cool" enough to start pulling the coke out the front opening.

The spray pipe was removed and the "beaver tail" inserted into the pulley. This twelve feet long pipe had what resembled the tail of a beaver at the end opposite the handle. The beaver tail, itself, about the size of the blade of a canoe paddle, turned down ninety degrees from the pipe handle. The idea was to hook a bunch of coke near the front of the oven with the beaver tail and pull it out of the opening, then gradually work it to the back and sides of the oven with each reach for more coke.

Grant and I took turns pulling the coke and shoveling it with a scoop shovel into the wheelbarrow, wheeling and dumping it into the railroad car. Dad helped us for about an hour that first morning before going to his own job on the tipple.

Some of the events of that first day which I'll never forget include: (1) we lost the wheelbarrow into the half-filled railroad car and spent twenty minutes getting it out of the still hot coke inside; (2) I got the hair above my forehead singed badly by getting too close to that hot oven; (3) we had not stopped for lunch when some of the workers around us had pulled two ovens and were on their way home; (4) I don't remember ever working that hard and sweating that much in the fifty years since then; (5) Grant mentioned that if we were ever tempted to ask dad for help in locating work again, we should review all our own options first.

Most of the other workers had gone home by the time we stopped for lunch. At that time we figured we were just a little over half way finished. Even cousin Frank Turner had pulled his one oven and gone home. After his shift at the tipple, dad came back for us as we were finishing up at 3 p.m.

By the end of that summer Grant and I were each pulling an oven by ourself. We got paid $8 for an oven. I don't remember much else about that summer when I was fifteen years old because we went to bed at 9 p.m. every night—just as the action was starting for the average teenager. Dad got us up every morning and would come down and help us for an hour before going to his regular job. Dad was wiry, but strong.

It was too bad, because we were now making good money but were too tired to spend it. I don't remember another summer when Grant and I prayed so hard for the summer to end and for school to start. This was not a fun job. In every other job I've had in life I found enjoyment, but when pulling coke is mentioned, I'll take the memories but don't ever want that job back.

The coke ovens continued operating until the Geneva Steel operation in Orem decided they could build their own coke producing ovens and have a more economical operation. In the late 1940s some of us toured the Orem plant and watched the mechanical operation of turning coal into coke. Thank heavens for technology.

During the great flood in Sunnyside in the late 1930s, the height of the coke ovens saved the lives of my older brother Dean and others working there as they sought higher ground as the flood chased them down the rows of ovens.

The coke ovens are now only memories. There's not much left of them. A miniature coke oven and the history of the coke ovens are now located at the Sunnyside Junction. But as for me, I'll remember the summer I spent "pulling coke" until those remaining behind file past and say, "My, doesn't he look natural."

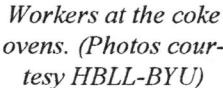

Workers at the coke ovens. (Photos courtesy HBLL-BYU)

COWS

When my granddaughters arrived after school for their favorite treats at grandmother's, on their way to the kitchen one of them piped up, "Gramps, do you know where dragon milk comes from?"

I knew the answer but in order to bond with my grand-kids, as my wife suggests, I answered, "From dragons "

"Wrong!"

As I get older and wiser, I'm learning that the youngsters will visit with old folks longer if you have a lot of questions and not very many answers. "Where does dragon milk come from?" I asked.

"From cows with short legs! I knew I'd get you on that one, gramps!"

The next sounds were the fridge and microwave doors as my grandkids made themselves at home in our kitchen. Children not growing up on a farm these days have no idea what we went through to obtain milk in the good old days in Sunnyside, even though we didn't live on a farm either.

By the late 1930s and early 40s, I was not big enough to milk the cows, but I was on the milk delivery route long before I reached the age of ten. The pints and quarts of milk sold at the company store had passed from our cows, through my dad's and brothers' hands, our kitchen and pantry, and ridden on the handlebars of our bikes to the store cooler.

The store didn't sell much milk in those days. If a family wanted a quart of milk, my dad put their name on the list and then they waited for a cow to 'freshen' or for a regular customer to move or cut back on the amount they wanted delivered.

When dad took over the company horse and mule barn in

1932, he purchased several milk cows. They were housed in a separate corral behind our house. Dad and my older brothers did the milking manually twice a day.

The equipment needed for milking cows consisted of a milking pail, a 2x4 "T" stool, a five gallon can, a bucket of grain and a lot of pull. The cow to be milked would migrate to the bucket of grain. The milker would then move rapidly to get the pail under the spigots, balancing his rear end on the stool and begin squeezing. The race was now on. The idea was to milk the cow dry before she finished the grain. If she finished first and was impatient, the milker's problems increased. You get the idea. At times when the little kids, Grant, Ella Ruth or I, wandered into the corrals at milking time, whoever was milking would turn the five gallon can lid upside down and fill it with warm milk and foam for us to drink. It was delicious!

When a cow had been milked, the fresh milk was poured into the five gallon can. When all of the cows had been milked, the five gallon can was taken to the kitchen for processing. The milk was poured through a clean flour-sack strainer into several large pans, then directly into the just-washed bottles, which seemed to fill up the kitchen at milking time. No plastic or cardboard containers in those early days—just pans and glass bottles.

The bottles of milk were delivered to our customers in metal carriers that held six one quart bottles each. The bike balanced better if there was a carrier of milk bottles on each side of the handlebars.

Some of the pans of milk were set on the pantry shelves for several hours until the cream came to the top. This thick cream was then scooped off with a cup and poured into half-pint bottles for delivery to the store or customers who had ordered it.

With no refrigeration, we and our customers drank a lot of uncool milk. We didn't mind, however, because many families had no milk at all. Our attempt at refrigeration in the summer was a wooden orange crate lodged in the pantry window, the part sticking outside covered by a gunnysack. The sack required cold water for evaporation and the cooling process (and I use that term loosely) to become active. Periodically, mother would remind one of the children in the kitchen to get a cup of cold water and step out on the porch and pour it over the gunnysack.

During the winter, if the milk set out on the porch overnight, by morning the cream had risen to the top and the frozen cream and milk had pushed the cap up creating a round column of frozen dairy product four or five inches above the top of the bottle. We could tell how cold it had been by the height of the frozen column. One customer told me that they left the bottle out overnight on purpose so they could get the frozen column of cream and eat it for dessert.

The bottle caps were round cardboard pieces about the size of a silver dollar. What's a silver dollar? It's about half the size of a pizza cutter. To uncap the milk bottle, you pulled on the tab on the top of the cap. If the tab pulled off before the cap was removed, which happened frequently, a sharp object and some prying would finish the job.

As youngsters we played tossing games with old, used milk bottle caps. Today's games with Pogs, discs the same size as the old bottle caps, are more varied and colorful, but they don't require near as much creativity.

One day while Ned was milking, Clair and a friend were standing nearby. Ned said to the friend, "This cow's milk will make your hair turn curly."

The friend, who sported a very short crew cut, leaned over while Ned shot a stream of milk onto his head. Some time later the boy's hair did grow out and was curly but, obviously, it had more to do with genes than pranksterism, since the other members in his family had curly hair, too.

During the summers, Grant and I were assigned the job of "herding the cows." After the morning milking, we would take the cows to a nearby grassy mountainside and let them graze for the day. If the cows didn't wander much, we could slip home for lunch and do other fun things like roll boulders down the mountain. A couple of the cows were gentle enough to ride both coming and going. The ride didn't beat walking, but the challenge was in balancing on the very broad top and trying to stay on board. We would return the cows to the corral in time for the evening milking.

With the advent of refrigeration trucks, display coolers, milking machines and other modern devices, not to mention strict regulations about pasteurizing and sterilizing, another time-consuming chore faded into history. And I don't miss it a bit.

But, as I pour skim milk over my morning cereal, checking the fat content, nutritional value, and cholesterol numbers on the carton, I wonder what memories my grandchildren will have fifty years from now.

THE CRIK (CREEK)

When I refer to the Crib in Sunnyside in some of my war stories, the kids raise one eyebrow and the grandkids laugh. The proper name may be creek, but to a Sunnyside native like me it will always be Crik.

When I learned that Secretary of the Interior Bruce Babbitt was going to lift the gates at Glen Canyon Dam to permit flooding, I wondered if we might do the same for the Sunnyside creek which has been controlled by a reservoir since the 1960s. Since that dam was built, the creek banks have eroded and some of the stream beds reworked, and shrubs and willows have just about taken over the creek, reducing it to a third of the size it was when I was a boy.

The George Whitmore family came from Texas in 1878 and began farming the land that is now the Sunnyside Park and part of the East Carbon City townsite, buying the water rights for twenty cubic feet per second, plus any water flowing in the sand and gravel of the stream bed, from the Grassy Trail Creek, which was the creek running through what would later become Sunnyside.

Most people these days don't fully understand how important water and water rights were to the early settlers of arid states like Utah. During the first half of this century the Utah Fuel Mining Company tried to get the water rights for the Sunnyside culinary supply and mine operations, without success. With a water problem for the community and mine, the Utah Fuel Company had to install pumps over the mountain in Range Creek after securing the water rights there from Preston Nutter. A steam boiler supplied the power to the lift pumps.

In several court battles between Utah Fuel Company and

the Whitmore family, the Whitmores always won and controlled the water rights until the late 1960s. At that time the Utah Fuel Company finally succeeded in buying the water rights and built a reservoir in the left hand Forks Canyon, thus controlling the floods that had caused problems for the residents of Sunnyside since the first ranchers and miners moved into the area.

To update my memory of the creek I recently returned to the place of my birth and visited parts of the creek that had played such an important part of our lives in Sunnyside. Things certainly have changed.

To make room for the coal operations after the houses in lower town were removed, the mine operators pushed the creek further to the north. There are now tall old trees in the stream bed. When I was growing up those trees were in the front yards of the houses in lower town.

Near where our house stood, the creek bed is, perhaps, fifteen feet across and ten feet deep. In the 1940s it was about seventy five feet from one bank to the other with the stream twenty feet or so below the banks. It is now all filled in and full of weeds and bushes. Now let's go back sixty years.

Every summer, about the time for school to let out, all of the young people in town would gather above the upper bridge across from the asphalt mill to build a swimming hole. The previous year's dam had washed out during the August cloudbursts and flooding. Everyone rushed to complete the dam and back up the water for swimming, knowing that in a couple of months the swimming season would end with the next big flood.

The dam building was an annual event with the young people urged by their parents to be careful so no one would get hurt or drown. Each year the kids listened with one thought in their minds—to get the dam built fast.

The big boys moved boulders from the nearby banks and positioned them in the creek bed, adding smaller rocks where they were needed. Others filled gunnysacks with dirt. These sacks were placed on the upstream side of the rocks to seal the holes in the dam. As the water backed up, more layers were added until the dam was eight to twelve feet high. Now the fun began.

Younger brothers who ventured near the water were often grabbed by one of the older boys and tossed into the water and told to either sink or swim. After fighting the water for a few seconds, gasping for breath and hollering as loud as we could, some compassionate soul would jump in and rescue us and take us to the other side to climb out. At least that was my first introduction to the swimming hole at about age six or seven. I might add, it was a great motivator for us youngsters to learn to swim. And we did.

The swimming hole had to be built above town because the sewer and waste water from those few houses which had inside bathrooms in upper town drained into the creek as it flowed through town. Even though parents told their kids to stay away from the creek in town because of the danger of contamination and disease, we still managed to find the sandy creek banks a great play area.

When Ella Ruth was about seven or eight years old she became sick with what they were afraid was Typhoid Fever. The doctor was concerned and our family were all very worried. She was very sick. The tests turned out to be negative for Typhoid Fever but she learned a hard lesson about heeding her parents' advice.

These days we're warned not to wade in or drink from streams high in the mountains because of the bacteria lurking there. Thank goodness THAT bacteria hadn't yet evolved in the old days or very few of us would have lived to maturity.

A bunch of us kids were playing in the creek behind Hansen's house one summer afternoon when one of our buddies got us involved in a science project. The bright idea he had learned was that gas would float on water. It sounded good to the rest of us. Our cousin, Frank, was with us and suggested we fetch a gallon can of gas from his dad's shed where Uncle Orson's mechanic son, Philip, always had some stored. We also got some matches and readied the experiment.

We poured the gallon of gasoline carefully onto the creek water and watched it slowly float downstream. When the can was empty, someone lit a match and threw it onto the gasoline topped water. When I've thought about this incident since, I've often considered what a magnificent sight it would have been if we had done this experiment when it was dark. The gas caught fire immediately, impressive flames shooting down the creek at least thirty feet. At that point it looked like the whole creek was being consumed by flames. The gas finally became diluted in the water and ceased burning. But our experiment was a great success. We did a lot of fun things when I was a kid.

Another time a group of us youngsters built a clubhouse along the creek among the Box Elder trees growing on the creek bank in front of Preston's house. Our buddy, Johnny Preston, worked right along side of us. We gathered 2 by 4s and other materials, including cardboard, and made a neat hut. Shortly after we completed it and were in the process of building a rafting pond in the creek next to it, it mysteriously burned to the ground. Rumor had it that dad and Johnny's father were involved. I wasn't sure, but mother said it was probably a good thing because it was too near the creek.

We then girded up our loins and built another clubhouse

in the canyon behind and a little south of the tennis court. Poor construction and boulders rolling down the mountain finally finished off this hut after a summer or two, but by then we were off to the next project. My brother Grant, Martin Rodosh and I built a dam in the creek in front of our house for rafting. The water backed up about twenty-five feet. We got old railroad ties for the raft, nailed them together and had some fun rafting. We watched that year as an August flood took the dam, raft and part of the creek banks and deposited them somewhere between Sunnyside and Wellington.

The great flood in 1936 caught our brother Dean, Bruno Della Corte, and other coke oven workers desperately climbing to the tops of the coke ovens to escape the flood waters. This flood enlarged the creek bed considerably and re-routed the road in several areas below town, besides taking a couple of houses and the back walls of the teachers cottage with it.

On a scout trip up the left-hand forks during the Christmas holidays, we walked on the frozen snow in the morning, but by late afternoon the snow had softened and each step put us over our knees in snow, making walking very difficult. Many of us worked our way down to the half-frozen creek and walked back to town down the middle of the creek. That was one cold, miserable scout hike, but the creek had become our friend once again.

When Pete Jones, who had taken over farming the Whitmore operations, was in court battling the Utah Fuel Company one more time over water rights a slick, educated lawyer asked this simple, uneducated man if he understood "what a second foot of water was?" Pete said he didn't, but added, "If the spring runoff is up to my horse's belly when we walk through the creek, then I'm getting my share of the water." He won once more.

The town has changed and the creek has changed, but my happy memories of growing up in Sunnyside and playing along the creek remain forever positive with me.

To this day, if you happen upon a group of strangers and they are having a good time and telling about the good old days and they mention the word "crik," you've happened upon a bit of history. When you hear the word "crik," you can trust them with your car or even loan them money on their smiles alone and it will be as good as any contract from an attorney, because they are probably Sunnyside old-timers. Go ahead and pronounce it crEEk, but it's still crik to those of us who had so much fun growing up in Sunnyside.

THE DEER HUNT

I was returning home on a Friday in mid-August when I noticed many campers, RVs and ATVs driving in the direction of rural Utah. I thought, "What a great family reunion and what fun they'll have if they can just find a place large enough to house them all." Most of them were in military colors. Then it hit me! These are not reunioners, but mighty bow hunters and the season is starting. The memories came flooding back.

When I was young growing up in Sunnyside, Labor Day signaled the start of that annual ritual known as the deer hunt. It was then that a young boy wished he was twelve or thirteen years old. That's when his training began. For the next six weeks males, old and young alike, would wear faded, torn and worn red shirts. Baseball type hats that had been brown all year would now have the top half that was reversible turned and, suddenly, the hat was red all over except the bill. Uncle Orson always tied a red bandanna around his cowboy hat and that did the trick for him.

Deer hunters are an interesting lot. In all my years of hunting, I've -never met a dedicated hunter who was ever too busy to miss the hunt. If there was leaky plumbing, animals to be fed or even predicted floods, mother and the kids could handle it. School was excused so teachers, too, could go on the hunt. If you were a truck driver, you parked the truck for ten days. No one missed the hunt. Broken leg? We'll help you on and off your horse. Too old? We'll prop you up in a chair on the ridge. Someone died? Schedule the funeral for Wednesday. No interested male missed the hunt.

Late September was the time to start putting the food into boxes and other containers. Never mind that we were just going for the weekend; pack plenty of food. Mormon leaders have long counseled that a year's supply of food should be on hand for each family. I now understand why. Six months of it was to go with the deer hunters and the remaining six months supply was to be used by the survivors if the hunter failed to return. All the hunters I ever knew returned, along with most of the food.

My younger brother Grant and I made our first pilgrimage to the hunting grounds when I was thirteen and he was twelve years old. We started out at daylight on Friday morning with many of the other men and boys in town. We were headed for Coal Springs, via the asphalt quarry and toward Range Creek. We rode horses, leading other pack horses, with the men telling hunting stories that were hard to believe. We tell the same stories to this day and they are still hard to believe.

We arrived at Coal Springs just before dark, sore, tired and hungry. Mother's lunch had long ago been consumed. Dad and the other adults made a fire, some supper, and rolled out the bedrolls in that order. As the tin dishes we'd eaten out of soaked in the cold spring water, the campfire nourished stories of bygone hunts and "the one that got away." We kids were tucked into our bedrolls as the old timers tried to top each other with a better tale.

It was still dark when I heard the men rustling around the fire. I don't remember sleeping but I guess we did. With just a thin sliver of daylight above the east ridge we got on the horses and began the trek to the "neat spot." I've gone to so many neat spots in over fifty years since that first hunt that I wonder if anyone ever went to a bad spot.

Hunters are eternal optimists. If it rains, that's great. Now the leaves will be soggy and not crackle underfoot and we can sneak right up to them. If it snows, that's even better.

Now we can track them as they leave fresh tracks in the snow. If the wind blows, even tornado force, that's even better. Now walking into the wind, the deer can't get your scent and you can walk right among them. If it happens to be 110 degrees, that's a good sign. The deer "shade up" in hot weather and you can get right to them before they move. And if the hunting is bad in this draw, I know right where they'll be heading out. I've never met a discouraged hunter. Dumb, yes. But discouraged, no way.

Old hunters permit kids to come along because they make good "drivers." A driver is one who goes down through the trees forcing the deer ahead while the old hunters sit on the ridge or near a clearing and wait for the "driven deer" to arrive.

On our first hunt I drove for a man who will remain nameless. I was moving up through the quakies when a shot was fired. He called out, "I got a big one! He's up above you about 100 feet!" I had heard stories around the campfire about wounded bucks attacking, so I got a quakie limb to defend myself and made my way from tree to tree. I poked along thinking if it was hit it would need time to bleed to death.

Arriving on the scene, I called out that it was a big one all right but no horns were in sight. The hunter was sure that I must be wrong. When he arrived at the killing site, he said that the one on the ground and a big buck must have changed places the one moment they were out of sight. I agreed as he got his knife out and began harvesting the hind quarters. We had fresh deer meat for the next several meals. In those impoverished days the meat was as important as the hunt itself.

Other highlights during my fifty years of hunting included: One year we saw and shot at 17 bucks and came home empty-handed. Dad shot the head off a perched crow. Another time he got a coyote about a half mile away. And, dad once got a deer in the neck at 300 yards, but on the close ones he rarely connected.

A few years after that first hunt, we could drive to the ridge above Coal Springs, so some rode horses and some drove vehicles. One year, Clair, Grant and I took dad's truck up during the second weekend of the hunt. A storm came up after we began hunting and we became lost. I was sure we were walking in the direction of the truck until we came upon our previous tracks in the snow and realized we were walking in circles. We happened upon Andy Anderson, who was hunting also. He pointed out the direction of our truck and we eventually found it. I learned something then. The shortest distance between two points is finding someone who knows directions.

One year I shot a nice buck on a hillside. While wondering how I was going to get it back to camp, Uncle Orson came by in his pickup truck with a rack on it and a horse in the back. He sized up the situation, opened the gate on the rack, dropped the tailgate and whistled to the horse. The horse backed out, Uncle Orson rode it to the deer, loaded the deer on the saddle and led the horse back to the truck. He tied the deer to the rack, led the horse to the back of the pickup, gave the horse a slap on the rump and the horse jumped back into the rear of the pickup. He shut the tailgate and rack gate, told me to jump inside the cab and we drove back to camp. I always liked hunting with Uncle Orson.

The best shot I ever made was years later after I moved my family to Richfield and had taken up bow hunting. We were getting set for the hunting opening day on the west mountain. I got a call from a lady in Gunnison who needed our moving services on that same opening day. I understood economics so I went to Gunnison with my moving van. Before leaving, my partners told me to leave my license and tag with them, "just in case."

At four in the afternoon the phone rang in Gunnison and the lady I was moving said, "It's for you." The voice on the other end said you just shot a nice two point buck. It will be in your backyard when you get home. Sure enough, it was there when I got home.

In church the next day one of my friends whispered, "Nice shot. It's not everyone who can lob an arrow from Gunnison and hit a buck on the west mountain." With a wink he said that they wanted to hunt some more and I would probably have to work, so they used my tag. He was right.

I've given up deer hunting, but I still recognize a good hunt when I see one, I thought to myself as I drove on home that Friday evening.

DISCRIMINATION

Not long ago we attended our class reunion. Forty-five years since we had graduated from high school. Among the returning graduates was Henry Washington. This was the first time we had seen him since our 1949 class graduation. As we introduced ourselves to Henry and reminded him of earlier experiences, he was having a hard time recalling most of us after all these years.

"It's easy for you to remember me since there was only one of me, but there were many of you." He repeated this more than once.

You see, Henry is black. The only black kid in our class and he was right, there were many of us. But even though there were no other blacks we were, nevertheless, a diverse yet gregarious group. We were second and third generation Greek, Italian, Japanese, Mexican, Scandinavian, German, Slavic, British and more. Besides this aggregation of nationalities, our class included a wide variety of religious affiliations. This diversity is rare in Utah but the norm in Carbon County and was the way of life in Sunnyside. In fact, the first two year period we lived in Provo, younger brother Grant came home from second grade the first day in our new school and said wonderingly, "everybody in my class is a Mormon." This was a new experience for him.

What was unique about our class and our town and our county was the fact that as diverse as it was in nationalities, religions, cultures and economic conditions, I don't remember any discrimination or problems between any groups of people. This lack of discrimination exists to this day.

Growing up in Sunnyside, my two best friends were Catholic but I don't remember that religion was ever discussed either between us or our parents. We respected each others' beliefs without commenting on their similarities or differences. We lived our religion and they lived theirs.

The creek that ran through the middle of town separated our socio-economic and nationality differences somewhat although, at the time, we all thought we were living in the best area in town. Sunnyside was divided into "upper town" and "lower town." Henry lived in a little two-room house at the very end of lower town.

Sunnyside was about two miles long and four rows of houses wide. Over the centuries, as the creek meandered through the canyon, its flooding had created flat areas large enough for each section of town. Although part of upper town, the northern most section was sometimes called "the asphalt" because in the middle of this section was the asphalt processing mill. The asphalt company superintendent and his family lived here. The town continued south across the upper bridge and under Sunnyside ledge and down through upper town. During World War I, Goblers Knob houses had climbed the hill behind the schoolhouse, but they were no longer there when I grew up. In this upper town section lived the mine superintendent and most of the mine supervisors and foremen and their families. Scandinavian and British names were predominant in upper town. Some of them were Lindsay, Erickson, Dennison, Hansen, Naylor, McMahon, Turner, Anderson, Watkins, Peacock, Preston, Jones, Lynn, Pressett, Swensen, Blackburn, Hunter, Morley, Durrant, Nelson, Ledger, Patterson, Hopkins, Gilligan, McCourt and Wycherly.

The upper town houses acquired inside bathrooms early on and many were one and a half stories high with two or three bedrooms each. Upper town was where the tennis court, schoolhouse, hospital, L.D.S. Church, company store, train depot, mine office, amusement hall and adjoining park were located. I was born in upper town, but that didn't last long.

Heading south and across the main bridge, on the west side of the creek and road and nestled at the foot of the mountain, was the post office and three houses, one of which was ours. This was in the area between upper town and lower town, which started just south of our house and the barn. The names in lower town changed to Italian, Greek, Slav, Spanish and Japanese. They included Rossi, DeAngeles, Fratto, Rhea, Baldi, Nichols, Della Corte, Eaquinto, Campagni, Boniquisto, Martinez, Vigil, Shiroto, Nitsuma, Farlaino, Bikakis, Kandaris, Tangaro and the aforementioned Washington.

Aside from the hotel, there were no story and a half houses in lower town. Just four room houses with outhouses behind them. Lower town contained the Greek Orthodox and Catholic Churches and the "Jap Hotel" where miners and laborers whose families were not with them lived. Once in awhile mine foremen and their families lived in lower town but, for the most part, this part of town housed simply hard working miners and their families.

We knew everyone in lower town as well as everyone in upper town and counted all of them as our friends.

When dad got his permanent job in Sunnyside, it was connected with his position as manager of the barn and corrals that housed the mine and coke ovens horses and mules. Our location next to the barn and across from the tipple was not quite in upper town and not quite in lower town. The nine houses from Salzetti's by the swinging bridge, including Nuzio's by the depot, down to our house were sometimes referred to as upper town and sometimes as lower town. I don't know that it made any difference to us. I do know, however, that we went from a one and a half story, two bedroom house to a small four room house. At least that's what my older siblings told me, since I was just thirteen months old when we moved. My last day in that four room house across from the tipple was during my furlough from the Air Force when I got married at age twenty one.

At the very south end of lower town, east of the creek and railroad tracks, were the sorry little two room houses where a couple of Mexican and Black families lived. As a boy, I delivered newspapers and gathered up empty beer bottles for their deposits in this area. The people were always very friendly and I never visited there without feeling a little sad at the conditions in which they lived. Henry lived there.

Because of unstable economic and working conditions, mine cave-ins and strikes, times were tough for nearly everyone in town. The creation of labor unions helped in the areas of economics and safety, but there were still plenty of poor people in Sunnyside. The coming of World War II and the demand for coal and coke for steel for the war effort, changed conditions for the better and everyone found steady employment. Two new towns, Sunnydale and Dragerton were erected below Sunnyside and they all three boomed during the 1940s and early 50s. Then the demand for coal softened again, coke making operations moved to the Geneva Steel Plant in Orem, and Sunnyside as we knew it faded into history. The houses are all gone now and a power station for the mine is now located where our house and the barn stood. Sunnyside is now what used to be called Sunnydale, and even some of the houses there are gone.

One event that I recall which bordered on discrimination happened one day when a neighbor kid, who was a couple of years older than me, grabbed my coat and began teasing me. In a moment of anger and frustration at my inability to regain my coat, I called him a "Wop." This was a slang term I had heard on occasion from men of every ethnic background. I didn't even know for sure what it meant but, to my young mind, it seemed like the appropriate name to call him. The kid then belted me a few times with his fists and I ran home crying.

Figuring that my parents would come to my defense and march right over to his house and read him the riot act, I explained the event in great detail right down to my calling him a "wop".

Mother gathered me in close and said, "He shouldn't have hit a kid smaller than him, but you should never use that word, or words like it, regardless of how mean someone is to you."

I didn't think mother was much of a defender at the time but later I realized the wisdom of her words. The next day that kid and I were friends and playing together again.

Times have changed and we've all changed with them. Now bald, Henry used to have hair. I used to deliver milk and newspapers. Ned, Grant, mother and dad used to be here with us. One thing that hasn't changed, however, is that former classmate Roland Vigil still plays his saxophone, but now in a band in San Francisco. I hope Henry won't wait another forty five years to attend another class reunion.

Looking back, I realize that things may not have been as rosy as I remember them, but if there was discrimination during my growing up years in Sunnyside, I failed to recognize it. It was just a great place to live. I don't recall any childhood enemies, including my coat-snatching neighbor.

Typical of the foreign families that migrated to America and became coal mining families are Rosa and Bill Eaquinto. Their friend, John Yachino, lived in a shack under a ledge in Slaughter Canyon. Bill and John worked the same shift so walked together to the mine.

(Photo courtesy the Eaquinto family.)

DOGS

Our town passed a leash ordinance not long ago. If you own a dog it must remain on your property or if you take it for a walk it must be on a leash. Bikers and joggers can now move throughout town without dogs nipping at their heels. I fervently agree with this law. Although I know many people in cities buy dogs for protection, as well as companionship, dogs have more freedom in the country where they can follow their natural instincts and run.

When I was growing up, Sunnyside must have had a "run loose" law—never was a dog on a leash or locked up in those days, and some of them should have been..

We had a wonderful old dog named Twist. Old Twist had a two inch scar on his back where the fur had been burned off when a neighbor threw scalding water on him. Twist was our protector and when anyone made threatening motions toward any of us kids, Twist would bare his fangs and stand ready to defend us with his life.

Twist was our 'buggy watchdog.' When each of us was the baby in the buggy going with mother, if she needed to run into the post office or elsewhere, Old Twist positioned himself under the buggy and growled menacingly if anyone came near. As we grew older if any of our friends pretended to attack us, Twist was between us and the friend in a flash. We all loved him dearly.

Old Twist was a scrapper. If a bigger dog wanted to fight, Twist was never one to back down. I called him away from fights more than once while growing up. We never worried about other kids or dogs when Twist was with us. And there were plenty of dogs in town to worry about. Sometimes the dogs ran alone and sometimes they ran in packs, but many of them were truly vicious. Evenings were bad times to be out alone when a pack of dogs was near.

Twist did have one dumb habit that I remember, but never did understand. He like to chase SOME cars. He chased about 10% of the cars in town. I don't know what was the qualifier—the color, the odor, or the year and model—but Twist only chased occasionally.

I was sitting on our front porch one day when one of the ten percenters came up the street in the opposite lane in front of our house. The chase and barking began. Just as Twist realized that he was losing another bout with an auto, he turned toward home and didn't see the car coming down the road in the opposite direction. Brakes squealed but it was too late. Old Twist was short enough that the bumper missed him, but the oil pan underneath the car caught him and he rolled end over end. When the car had passed over him, it looked like the fox and hare battle in one of those TV wildlife documentaries—just a ball of fur, feet and barking. When he stopped rolling, Twist hobbled back home and sat on the porch for several days, licking his bumps and bruises. He was a little wiser as he was healing, but he never did get the deeper message since he was back trying to catch the ten percenters a week later.

When I was about eight years old, Old Twist slowed down and began moving around the yard and porch with less and less enthusiasm. Dad realized what was happening but explained it to me by saying Twist must be sick. After a while Old Twist died. He had been our gentle friend and protector and the most intelligent animal we ever knew. We were sad and long-faced for several days after Old Twist went to that happy chasing-highway in the sky.

But the population of Sunnyside dogs continued to grow. Salzettis had two big, mean Doberman Pinschers. They could run the 100 yard dash in four seconds flat and I believe their bite could have ripped an arm or leg off. Raymond Salzetti often said, "They don't bite and they won't hurt anybody." But we knew better. If you took the swinging bridge route from upper town down to our house, the route took you past the Salzetti yard and you always said a silent prayer that the dogs were locked up.

Ella Ruth still remembers with a shiver the time she was coming home from elementary school and had just crossed the swinging bridge when Salzetti's dogs, running loose, spotted her. The race was on. It's amazing how fast legs can move when terror is the motivator. Screaming at the top of her lungs, she beat the snarling giants by less than five yards as she ran into Durrant's yard and slammed the gate behind her. About that time, Raymond emerged from his house and whistled and the dogs, obeying their master, trotted home. The next day in class Raymond reminded Ella Ruth that the dogs wouldn't really have hurt her, but she didn't believe him for a minute. This was the very reason we used the main street to get home more often than the shorter swinging bridge route while Salzetti's had those dogs.

Prestons had an old Cocker Spaniel named Snooper. In dog years he was at least one hundred years old. He would lay on their front porch and let out a slow, deep growl as you knocked on their front door. But he never got up to check you out. The only time I ever saw him move was when he heard dinner scraps being scraped into his bowl, and even then every movement was sluggish.

Grant and I had paper routes in our early teen years. I delivered to upper town and he delivered to lower town. A bike and paper route gave you two advantages when encountering menacing dogs. If you saw the dog coming you could dismount the bike on the opposite side and keep the bike between you and your four-footed tormentor. Also, a rolled-up newspaper gave you some leverage, especially when you brought it down full-force between the threatening dog's eyes. A retreating, yelping dog was one of my favorite sights.

Once on Grant's route, a dog bit him on the leg. When he finished delivering his papers, he came looking for me and reinforcements. Several of our friends with bikes agreed that the dog must be punished for its deed. We all found heavy wooden sticks and rode to lower town looking for the guilty critter. As we rode we talked about how that dog would look when we were through with it. Thankfully we never found the dog. Several other dogs barked and chased after us as we went by but none looked like the dog Grant had described.

Emile Zupon, who lived up by Tubby Jones's house, had a small dog, but it was the meanest dog on the route. One day when my bike had a flat tire I had to walk to deliver the papers. After I hit the Zupon porch with a three point long shot with the paper, I could hear the familiar, high-pitched bark off in the distance but headed my way. Without my bike for protection, I took off at full tilt. It's tough to run at full throttle when dragging a loaded paper bag over your shoulder. The closest, safest place was the railing around Jones's porch. I beat the little beast by about four steps. I was standing on the four-feet high railing, swinging wildly, when Mrs. Jones opened her door and asked what I was doing.

"I'm trying to keep from getting bitten," was my excited reply.

She then turned to the dog and said, "Shoo! Go on home!" The dog quit barking, turned and ran home.

When I got home I told dad about my experience and why I needed to get the bike fixed pronto. He said that a dog can tell when you're scared by the smell you give off and by the fear in your eyes. He added, "Just don't be scared and you'll be okay."

This is the kind of advice that dads give. I've given some myself. You can't just turn off fear. I have dog fear to this day.

I had a similar encounter with a dog as an adult professional Scout leader. Clint Tanner of Fremont invited me to bring some merit badge cards on the next trip "over the mountain." Clint lived in a pioneer home with foot thick rock walls.

My fear of dogs had taught me to have several escape plans whenever the possibility of a dog attack might occur. This possibility can happen often in Wayne County. I parked in front of Clint's home. I left the car door open and the fence gate open also in case of sudden need to vacate.

Past the point of no return, I recognized the familiar snarl of a big, angry dog. Too late to make it back through the gate to my car! I ran to Clint's front door and as I hit it in full stride, I pulled the screen door behind me as tight as possible. I was pressed between the screen door and the front door. It's hard to knock on a door in this position but I did it. Thank heavens for thick-walled pioneer homes. I tumbled into the front room when Clint opened the door.

Like all dog owners, Clint said Old Sport wouldn't hurt a fly. I promised Clint a merit badge pamphlet if he would walk back out to the car with me. I was out the 35¢ for the pamphlet but it was well worth it.

When I expire I'll know I've gone to heaven if I don't see or hear any signs of dogs anywhere. Unless, of course, Old Twist is there. Then I'll know I'm in heaven's highest realm.

DRUMS, BANDS
AND CAT-SCANS

July is parade month. I like parades. I like holiday parades for two special reasons. They have flags and bands. For an old patriotic, ex-scouter, and a former band member, nothing brings me to attention like the flag coming by in a parade followed by the bands. I have a special spot in my heart for the bass drummer in a parade since I was one once.

Sometimes I called it a 'base' drum but it was really a bass drum. The dictionary calls bass: lowest part in music. And that describes my relationship to that particular musical instrument during my growing years. Let's start from the beginning. . .

My mother scrimped and saved and acquired a trumpet by the time her first-born was ready to join the band at the Sunnyside School. Dean played the trumpet. Then my sister Winnie played the trumpet in the band. Brother Ned played the trumpet, too. While brother Clair was waiting for the trumpet to become available he played the French horn, then the trumpet. Sister Ella Ruth did some time with the French horn while waiting for the handme-down trumpet.

Next it was my turn but we had moved and there was no trumpet available so I began on the school owned French horn in the Fourth Grade. We were living in Provo at the time. We returned to Sunnyside in time for me to enter the Fifth Grade. The French horn stayed behind. Younger brother Grant was just beginning to learn how to play the trumpet and no French horn was available so Mr. Pisa, the band teacher, asked me to learn how to play the bass drum.

When I took up the drum rather than the trumpet, mother

realized right then that our family would not be invited, as was Joshua, to re-enact the Joshua and Jericho story in the Old Testament. Remember that one, where with SEVEN trumpets and a lot of shouting, the walls came tumbling down? We could probably handle the shouting part all right, but without SEVEN trumpet players we would come up short on the rest of it.

I began my lifetime affair with the bass drum. I was a bit under five feet high. The bass drum in those days was about three feet high and eighteen inches wide. When we took up marching, I could barely see over the drum. A small bass drummer in a marching band develops strong back muscles early in life.

Year after year I played the bass drum. One note is all I hit and I never did know the name of the note. You can't tell the difference between a half note and an eighth note on a bass drum. Now the snare drummers got to rumble and play a lot of different rhythms, but a bass drum?! Once you've mastered the first beat, it never changes.

When it came to grading, each band member got a grade based on attendance and musical skill. How do you grade a bass drummer who has a perfect attendance record? I never got worse than a B. But, on the flip side, I never got better that a B either. I guess you could say, as far as band was concerned I was about a B average.

Band teachers are great motivators and positive thinkers when it comes to a Band Meet. We went to one or two in Price every year and we always came home with a handful of certificates rating us in the various areas of: marching skills, difficulty of tunes, clearness of tones, every member in harmony, etc. you get the idea.

And the rating went from Superior to AAAA to Excellent to Outstanding to Remarkable to A Plus to None-Better.

The worst you could do would be to get a rating of Above Average. Everyone went home from these band contests thinking that their band was the Meet's greatest.

During my Sophomore year, we moved back to Provo for another two year stay. My band teacher was Mr. Sutherland. He was the same man who had started me on the French horn six years earlier. The next year he got a job at B.Y.U. and we got a new teacher, Mr. Isaacson.

Mr. Isaacson was a John Phillip Sousa fan, but he wasn't fanatic about it. He brought in an overture or two and some other musical newcomers. I remember trying to stay with his beat on Khachaturian's "Sabre Dance." We were both at full speed and once in awhile we were together.

Mr. Isaacson doubled my musical skills. He introduced me to an instrument called the triangle. A triangle is like a bass drum in a lot of ways. There is just one note to master and there is no chance to get off-key. Now I could play two instruments, but that was the extent of my musical talents.

From Provo, it was back to Carbon High in Price for my Senior year. Mr. Williams, who had been my band teacher from the time Mr. Pisa left for a job in Salt Lake, was still at it and welcomed me back. I wondered who was the bass drummer for the two years I was gone? Maybe they didn't have, or need, one. One thing about it, wherever I went I always had a position with the band. With trumpets, you practiced and worked to be First Chair. Not so with the bass drum. If anyone had come along wanting the job, I would have given it to him or her without a fight. I would have taken study period in a heartbeat. But I always showed up at the band room to do my thing.

Back to the parade. Bass drummers these days have got it made. Have you seen the size of some of those drums? And those marching bands on TV during the football season?

Notice the bass drum. Some are no larger than a king-sized pizza, and not much thicker either.

When I got my high school diploma in 1949, I thought the band room was history. But when I was registering for Carbon Jr. College the next August, Mr. Williams was there and asked if I could come and play the bass drum for at least one more year. I could and did. The college and high school band was one and the same in those days. I was now one of the older band members.

I could be wrong, but as I recall, I was back playing the bass drum during my second year at Carbon Jr. College, too. When I got to B.Y.U. a few years later, I stayed clear away from the music department. I learned later that I had no need to worry because the B.Y.U. band had three or four bass drummers and when they high-stepped it across the football field, I could see that my physical condition would keep me out of the band. I didn't even want to move that fast anymore. While earning a degree in Elementary Education there in the 1950s, a children's music class was required so I signed up. The teacher? Mr. Sutherland. Small world.

You don't hear the old John Phillip Sousa marches so much anymore since band music has gotten modern and has a different beat to it. I've asked my wife to have the marches playing in the background at my Viewing, but I'll bet she won't. I still enjoy them on my tapes as I'm driving around the country. No one at a truck stop would recognize them, but I'll take a good, rousing march over a Willie Nelson tape any day.

One event I remember to this day is the time we first started marching when I began playing the drum in the Fifth Grade. Because I could barely see over the drum and had to take giant steps to keep up with the Ninth and Tenth Graders, I stepped into a chuck hole in the street and stumbled. As I went down, the drum stopped me from hitting the road but I was strapped tight to it and began to roll over the top. Just when I got to the lowest point (the phrase these days is: "where the rubber meets the road") I put my hands in front of my face. The drum beater (that is, the stick with a sheep-skin ball on the end, not the guy holding it) met my face on one side and the road on the other side and I was saved from a broken neck or getting crushed. The other band members broke up with laughter and Mr. Pisa gave us the rest of the period off. I was a little more careful where I stepped after that.

Anyone wanting to play the 'base' drum all the years that I played it is a candidate for a CAT-SCAN. At best, he has one oar out of the water.

ETHICS, LYRICS AND POLITICS

"Eclectic: Selecting or made up of what seems best of varied sources. That describes growing up in Sunnyside, all right. Sunnyside was made up of diverse and multi-faceted individuals who worked and lived together in the best interests of community and democracy. Of all the counties in Utah, Carbon was, and is, the most heterogeneous. And in Sunnyside, we were many religions, many nationalities and many cultures but we were one in expectations and ethics.

"Have a good time," were not only the last words mother said as we youngsters went out the door for an activity, but this same message was repeated by other mothers to their youngsters as they left the house. Parents expected children to have a good time in lawful and ethical ways. Expectations and values were well-defined but I don't remember spending much time discussing them with my parents. They didn't preach or nag but we all knew we were to behave in morally acceptable ways. The expectations were about the same in all families regardless of ethnic or religious persuasion. There were community expectations. We were united as a community.

If it were possible, I'd transpose my grandkids from their present locations and conditions back to the Sunnyside I knew as a youngster in the 1930s and 40s. I believe our generation was blessed beyond any other generation in history. We were poor in earthly goods but rich in community values. Families looked after their own, heroes were good examples and, more often than not, family members and a person's word was his bond.

My grandkids live in a different world. A world threatened with drugs, gangs and violence. Movies, TV and the printed word contain more violence and flagrant immoral behavior than we could have ever imagined in our growing years. A contract and lawyer are necessary for too many transactions and kids are lucky if they have a support system at home and rules to follow.

For the generations before us, harsh living conditions made physical survival a way of life. For my grandkids, physical survival is fast becoming a way of life again, though in much different ways. For my generation, survival was only a word used in connection with disease, a bad accident, a World War II battle, or to describe those not cut from the team.

In the Sunnyside of old, group fun was the norm. Dances, parties, sleigh rides, ice skating, weiner and potato roasts were all group activities. If food was involved, everybody brought some. Parents were involved in every step and were partners in all our endeavors. Our mothers were as busy as mothers of any generation, but their childrens' welfare was a top priority. New babies were welcomed and loved.

Transportation was a common necessity for all of us. If you had a vehicle, you offered rides to others. If you needed a ride, it was safe to thumb one. Without a car, thumbing a ride was a common practice. Drivers were not afraid to stop and give you a ride. Buses were uncommonly used. Bus drivers took passengers other than their regulars if they needed a ride. Insurance, government regulations and lawsuits did not dominate actions.

If you needed money, you were expected to work for it. In the summers we young people who wanted to work could find jobs. The job was usually hot, tedious, back-breaking and low paying but it was always welcome. Money was not easy to come by and most of our activities did not require much money. Economics did not drive our behavior. When we were old enough and responsible enough to own a car (always used and needing repairs), a ten minute visit with dad and the banker would do it. Bankers, dads and kids were friends. The banker and dad expected the young car owner to make the required payments. A handshake and signature completed the deal. Dad's signature was collateral enough. You got two things with the purchase of a car—payments and more friends.

If our group met at the bowling alley Gus Burdis, the manager, became our proxy father. If we wanted to dance, he'd let us move things around to make room. He expected good behavior from us and he got it. Fifty years later, Gus is still a good friend.

Frank Ellis, the local sheriff, was another friend to us kids. None of us wanted to see a red light in our rearview mirror but I don't remember him giving any of us tickets. He would stop us for a "prayer meeting" if we were not obeying the rules but he never abused his authority. Sunnyside was full of examples, expectations and ethics.

Today there is not only a generation gap in ethics, but in music, too. So much of today's music is not only ear shattering but many of the lyrics are offensive and degrading. Responsible parents who tune in to the songs their children are listening and dancing to, are shocked by the violence and obscenities.

Dancing to the melodies in the 1930s and 40s was relaxing and romantic. Today's dancers need both chiropractors and chaperones. My wife got a little irritated with me when I told my son who plays with a rock band group that his music sounds just like the transmission of my truck when it went out. She counseled me that this was no way for a father to bond with his youngest child. My son just smiled and said words to the effect that I'm clear out of touch.

And maybe he's right. Growing up in the 1930s, and 40s, our favorite music came from the Big Bands. Who will ever forget swinging to Glenn Miller's "In the Mood," or dancing close to his "Moonlight Serenade?" And what about the warm glow when you were holding hands with your favorite girl as you listened to a sweet rendition of "Stardust?" Harry James's trumpet could keep the sleepiest awake and whistling. Les Paul and Mary Ford and their echoing guitars was a big change in music in our young days, but it made the listening that much more enjoyable.

Gone is the Saturday night Hit Parade where the Top Ten songs of the week were played; the jukeboxes where a quarter would get you five tunes; and radio stations that only played music you could sing along with or tap your toes to. As we listened to those wonderful Big Bands all of us, kids, parents, grandparents, knew the songs and would often sing along.

Gone, too, are the hometown orchestras which played for our Saturday night dances in the school gym. The orchestra was made up of amateur musicians who were self-taught, had learned music in the school band programs or taken piano lessons from Mrs. Hansen, but their music was sweet to the ears. Everyone in Sunnyside, young and old alike, came to the dances and enjoyed dancing and visiting and just listening to the music.

Also gone are the summer night teen dances at the tennis court where Jimmy Eaquinto and his accordion kept our feet happily moving; or jitterbugging to the jukebox at the confectionery.

It's true I'm out of touch with today's music. But, if I could do it, I'd take my kids and grandkids back to the 1930s and 40s where our music volume didn't pin us to the wall when we walked into a room, and where the lyrics may have been artless but they didn't insult our sensibilities, either. I guess if we have junk food today it's only natural that we have junk music also.

But all is not lost. I still have my tapes of the music we grew up with. And whenever I need a breather I just slip in some of my Big Band or Ragtime or Bluegrass music and return once again to those sweet-sounding Sunnyside days.

As I listen to my tapes and reminisce about growing up, there's always one memory that brings a smile. While we went to different churches and conversed in different languages in our homes, the one thing all of us in Sunnyside had in common was our politics. Until World War II brought in new families and new thinking, every single one of us was a Democrat. We children had been well-versed at home and we were as elated when Franklin D. Roosevelt beat Wendell Wilkie as our parents were. Even today, where Utah is the most Republican state in the nation, Carbon is the most Democratic County.

Dad would have enjoyed cable TV channels, but I know he would have used the channel changer when it was time for the Republican Convention. I didn't even know a Republican until my uncle came to visit us. Dad couldn't understand how he could be a good church member AND be a Republican. I was eight years old before I learned that United Mine Workers Leader, John L. Lewis, and President F.D. Roosevelt were not members of our family. When we said our prayers at night we included them along with each member of our family.

There were only two times that I can remember dad questioning my judgement. One was when I bought a Plymouth car and the other was when I voted for Eisenhower. The brand of a car was like dad's politics—we only drove Chevrolets. Dad's brother's son was a Chevy salesman and mechanic. We were loyal family members and loyal family members always bought from other family members.

Dad and his political faith were sometimes a bit of a contradiction. For example, when dad was elected a County Commissioner as a Democrat, he wanted people OFF welfare, not ON it. Not a common Democratic tenet. He would call family members when someone applied for welfare and tell them they should be taking care of this family member, not having the government do it. Also at this time he observed that during the winter, the road department always sent out equipment in pairs. When asked about this practice, he was told that they went in pairs during the winter in case one piece of equipment should break down. Dad countered that most homes now had telephones and that as long as he was a commissioner, and only one piece of equipment was needed for a job, that is all that would go, and if it broke down the operator was to visit a house nearby and ask to use the phone. This, and the fact that dad worked to close down all the bars in Carbon County that were serving liquor by the drink, which was against the law, made dad's Commission service a one-term position.

I once asked him why he was a Democrat. He told me about the times in his early married years when he would go to the mine and wait most of the day only to be told that there was no work that day. He had known the mines when safety was not something the management cared about, and he related stories of when miners had been killed in the mine and their widows and children got nothing, not even a company-owned house to live in any longer. He added that the Democratic party had been responsible for getting the unions organized and the unions had been responsible for job security, decent wages and safer working conditions.

With Roosevelt's programs during the New Deal the country got moving again and those with no special skills, like dad, were part of the labor force that kept this country moving. I can understand his trust in John L. Lewis and Franklin D. Roosevelt. Perhaps they would have been my heroes, too, under similar circumstances.

Dad voted the straight Democratic ticket every election. His vision for the Democratic party was to help the less fortunate while reining in the expansion of government and increased taxes. It was a vision that was not to be. But he did his personal share of helping the less fortunate by giving fruit and dairy products to those in need when he sold milk in Sunnyside and later peddled fruit after he retired and moved to Provo.

He was a good Democrat, but if he were around now I wonder what he would think of the present day party agenda. He and the church he loved taught and practiced self-reliance and that assistance should only be temporary. Washington could use his values today.

Democrats and unions will always be synonymous with Carbon County and my memories of Sunnyside. Most of us who grew up there and later moved away no longer stick to any one straight party ticket. And yet, we'll never forget what the Democratic party meant to those who were there before us.

FLIES

There were two kinds of flies that I encountered while growing up in Sunnyside. There was the fly which was a winged insect; and the fly that was a well-hit softball, some-times elevated to the status of a home run. This memory deals with the activities of the winged tormentor kind.

Two events ushered in my favorite season during my growing up years. One was that dad no longer needed to make fires in the stove that was used just for heating. The other was that we were to shut the screen door tight since flies were now in season.

Flies are funny little critters. They are slow learners. They will fly against a window a million times and still not get the message. In those days, good screen doors were hard to come by. You usually got a new one with a new house, then it was downhill after that. You could tell the age of each Sunnyside house by the number of holes and patches on the screen doors.

Our back screen door had a hole in it which was a regular airway trail for flies, both large and small. They could always tell when mother was cooking and what was cooking. Flies have good noses.

Fly swatters were different in those days. Nowadays you can get a color coordinated plastic swatter to go with any decor. They stay flat and look nice. The old swatters had mesh wire with a black wire handle. In Salt Lake City once I saw some with a white handle for sale, but we certainly did-n't have money to waste on one of those when our old one still worked fine. The swatter hung on a prominent nail, usu-ally near the door.

In those early days we shared food with the flies more

than we do now. Now, if a fly alights, we discard that portion of the food. In those days flies often stayed long enough to eat and deposit their eggs. Today's youngsters don't recognize the word "fly-blown." They wouldn't recognize a gunny-sack cooler either.

My mother hated flies and back then she really knew how to herd them. She was great at grouping them for their flight out of our kitchen. When there were more flies inside than out, she would pick up her flour-sack dishtowel and stand with her back to the wall opposite the back door. One of us kids would be assigned to stand outside the screen door and wait for the word. The fly drive was about to begin.

Swinging her towel toward the ceiling corners in rapid motions, mother would begin moving across the kitchen. She kinda reminded me of a middle-aged, pom pom waving, high school cheer leader leading the fight song. Usually increased buzzing would accompany the swoosh, swoosh, but on occasion mother would say, Shoo, shoo with her arms and body in synchronized motion as she moved across the room.

As she neared the door, between "shoos" she called out, "Open it now!" With the screen door open and the activity at full speed, every last buzz was accounted for and out the door. Mother then returned to her gentle, calm movements and continued her work. On hot summer days this ritual was repeated several times.

Another thing I don't see anymore is fly paper. It seems to have gone the way of wire swatters. Fly paper came in a small tube about the size of a shotgun shell. For the uninitiated, a shotgun shell is about the size of a large lipstick tube or, if you don't wear makeup, about the size of a 2C flashlight battery.

We bought the fly paper tubes at the Sunnyside Store or in Price. Because of the run on them with the first hint of summer, we nearly always got ours in Price when dac went for a load of livestock feed. We always got two. One for each room in our house with an outside door.

It took great skill to activate fly paper. On the top of the tube was a loop of string that was attached to a thumb tack or small nail driven into the ceiling. Only big folks could activate fly paper. The activator would stand on a kitchen chair, hook the string to the nail in the ceiling and carefully pull down on the tube.

As the tube was pulled down, the two inch wide paper would uncurl. The paper strip had brown, sticky, fly-attracting glue covering both sides. This fly paper strip extended about two and a half feet down from our eight feet high ceiling. The paper enticed flies and when they landed on it, it was lights out for them.

With their stuck buddies trying to buzz them off, the rest of the flies continued to gather on the fly paper. (Remember what I said about them being slow learners?) The buzzing would be very loud at first then finally come to dead s lence. Pardon the pun.

One strip of fly paper was usually hung above the kitchen table because that was where the most action was. I remember one special incident involving dad and fly paper.

Dad was helping mother one evening with supper. Now they call it dinner, but back then the evening meal was called supper. Dad was maneuvering around the table dish ng up the potatoes when he leaned too far across the table. During this lapse in judgement, his hair brushed against the fly paper.

As he jerked his head back, the string holding the fly paper broke and the fly paper began to attack him. He dropped the pan of spuds on the table and began quoting scripture. I could see that this battle was to the finish with only one survivor. Mother jumped to dad's side and greatly increased the odds in his favor.

It was much like a deep sea diver battling a mad octopus. Mother finally got him untangled and, lifting the cookstove lid, eliminated the ceiling creature. She got dad to the kitchen sink (it was the only sink we had) and, with some scrubbing, got him presentable enough to join us for supper. Mother always did have a cool head.

Needless to say, we did without fly paper in the kitchen for the rest of that summer. We can be glad of the EPA, FDA and OSHA or we might still be hanging fly paper every summer.

THE FOURTH OF JULY

It's funny how we humans evolve and then return to our beginnings again. Take the 4th of July, for example. My first experience was as an unknowing, uninterested spectator. You see, I was being pushed in the buggy (now we have strollers and babies can sit up and see out) over to the Amusement Hall lawn where the races were about to begin.

Later, as a youngster not old enough to compete, I became an interested spectator for a year or two. Then I evolved into a participant, an active participant, as you'll soon see.

Now, in my declining years, I'm just an interested spectator again, but I can feel the uninterested bones in my body evolving and taking me back to the beginning.

If you stay in small Utah communities, you'll find two things about the 4th of July that never change. They are the 5 a.m. dynamite blasts and the fireworks. Why they set off the dynamite at 5 a.m. to signal Independence Day is a mystery to me. Even though I've been in the military, I still can't figure out why the 4th of July has to begin that early in the morning. The day is long enough anyway without having to start it at 5 a.m. But, it's either get used to it or move to the city. I'll take the noise once a year; I've seen the city. Now, when I was a boy . . .

July 4th was a big deal in Sunnyside. It usually began about mid-June with Mike Fratto lighting packages of firecrackers and throwing them from the store porch late each afternoon. This was a fun event and as a youngster I tried to be near the store for this excitement every day. There were times when he would even let me light some of the firecrackers.

Then came the day of the 4th, itself, with the dynamite blast followed by young men with their trumpets on the mountain peaks at both ends of town playing reveille and taps. Those sweet notes carried far and clear over that early morning air. After the dynamite and trumpets had made sure we were awake, and we had finished our chores, we put on our second-best overalls and shirts and headed for the action at the lawn in front of the Amusement Hall.

Everyone in town gathered here for the excitement. Dad and other community-minded volunteers had arrived at the lawn much earlier to get things ready for the events that started about 10 a.m.

Races were the highlights of the day's activities. We competed by ages. I can hear it now. John Preston would stand in the middle of the big lawn with all the competitors waiting at the south end. "All those up to age four, line up! Ready, set, GO!" And the races were on. The winner got a dime, but so did everyone else. John and other Union members, including dad, wore carpenter aprons with big pockets in the front and the pockets were filled with dimes.

Those who fell during the race got a footprint or two up their backs, but the dime took all the pain away.

"Now, five and six-year-olds!" And another race was on the way. Parents and other family members lined both sides of the partitioned-off raceway cheering on their favorites.

Older youngsters learned how to work the system. If the group of racers was large enough, and you were fast enough, you could usually visit two guys wearing aprons and pick up an extra dime. If you got caught, it was embarrassing as someone would yell out, "Hey, Turner kid, you've already got your dime!" I'm glad I never did this.

Soon it was time for the older teenagers and adult races. My sister, Winnie, and dad were both very fast. They won often. In fact, dad used to take Winnie to Wellington, too, to compete in the races there and she usually beat everybody else in her age group in both towns. From the time you were old enough to compete in the teenagers and adults races, only the first three winners received money. But by then it was worth the quarter to try and be one of the winners. A quarter went a long way then.

As soon as all the racers had worked up a good sweat, it was time for the specialty races. One of my favorites was the three-legged race. This took more coordination than speed. Two participants would take off their belts and wrap them around their inside legs securing them together. One belt went above the knees and the other below. Then, at the sound of the race leader's command, the race was on. It was a good race if three couples made it to the finish line without falling down. If you fell once or twice, you were still a strong contender so it was up and on your way again since in some of these races all of the participants stumbled and fell at least once.

Then it was the gunnysack race with your feet in a gunnysack up to your waist and you hopping like mad to the finish line. There were very few finishers in this race.

Finally there was the wheelbarrow race with one person holding the other's legs like the handles of a wheelbarrow and pushing him along and the other doing the running on his hands. If your overalls and shirt were not stained and dirty before this, this race completed the job as your arms gave out and you nose-dived into the grass and dirt.

Free ice cream cones and pop rounded out the morning's events. After sharing jokes, laughs and handshakes, everyone left to change into their well-worn everyday clothes to head for their separate family activities.

Often we would gather up our home-made root beer and

lunch mother had prepared for us and meet other families up at Pasture Canyon, Box Springs, The Forks, or down below town near Pete Jones' ranch. Baseball and other activities, along with plenty of good food, or a weiner roast finished up the afternoon.

We always had to get home before dark. We had cows to feed and milk, horses and chickens to feed, milk to deliver, and wood and coal for the stove to carry in. And these were "the good old days."

At night we'd sit on the front porch setting off our remaining firecrackers, finishing the evening with sparklers and Roman Candles mother and dad had bought for us in Price. It didn't get any better than this.

As older teenagers we, at times, would bring "our girls" along with the family, holding hands when no one was looking. We'd also bring along the stray friends who didn't go with their families. We always attracted friends of all ages at our family gatherings.

The last Sunnyside 4th of July celebration I can remember participating in was when the events had moved down to the area behind the Sunnydale store. I remember that one well because I remember Winnie, grown-up by this time but still the fastest, falling when she was way ahead of everyone else; dad winning his race; and Martin Rodosh and I winning the tennis doubles match and each getting a silver dollar. Inflation moved a little slower in the old days.

The holiday is the same these days but some things have gotten larger—like my family! Nowadays on the evening of July 4th, after watching the parade downtown in the morning and the family picnic during the afternoon in our backyard, grandma Ardyth pops big baskets full of popcorn, and our family and friends gather in our front yard as we wait for the town-sponsored fireworks display on the west hills. Our front lawn has one of the better views. After the town fireworks, our older kids bring out their own fireworks and the fun really begins..

I can always tell when July 5th has arrived. I begin the day by gathering the spent sparkler wires from the lawn, and finish by deciding that the black snake marks on the cement driveway will just have to wear off naturally since they won't come off with the hose.

With all my kids and grandkids and their endless energy, there's really no chance that I'll end up as an uninterested spectator on July 4th, no matter how old and tired I get.

"GOOD OLD GOLDEN RULE DAYS"

In the history of Utah, schools have always held an important place. In the late 1890s when work in Sunnyside began in earnest, those early miners and asphalt workers wanted schooling for their children. Once the L.D.S. chapel was completed in 1900, it was used to accommodate school age children during the week days. A wooden, two-story school building was not completed until the following year. This first school had a bell tower and the bell was rung at the start of the school day. The building had no running water or bathroom facilities and the children used the customary out-houses. This school was heated by wood and coal stoves and a few years later, caught fire and burned to the ground. Another, smaller school for grades one through three was built in lower town after Sunnyside was incorporated, but was only used for a few years.

In the meantime, a new school building was constructed of stone, cement and coke breeze at the site of the original building in upper town. Coke breeze was similar to the use of sand in today's concrete construction. This school was a square, two-story structure with four rooms on each floor. In the 1920s this school again caught fire and burned, leaving just the four walls standing. The L.D.S. chapel was again put into service as a temporary school.

Because of increasing enrollment and the need for class-es beyond elementary grades, a new school building was constructed. The original four standing walls became the out-side of the west wing of the new building, but two basement rooms and a furnace room were added. In addition to the four rooms on the first floor, a principal's office and small storage room were added. On the top floor, a gymnasium and two classrooms made this wing complete. A similar two-story matching east wing was built at the same time. It contained four rooms on each floor. But this new addition also contained two indoor lavatories, one for girls and one for boys. An upper and lower enclosed walkway connected the two wings together.

Now the school could house students in grades one through nine. In the late 1920s, students in nearby farming community, Kiz, and seventh through ninth grade students from Columbia were bused to this Sunnyside school.

In 1931 the student population began decreasing and grade ten was added to the curriculum. In 1932 the eleventh grade, consisting of eleven students, was added. The School Board could make these additions because the Depression was causing families to leave the area looking for work elsewhere.

At this time, students wanting to Complete their high school work had to live in a school district dormitory in Price, paying for their room and board. During these years many high school age students left school because economic conditions required them to work full time, or work on the family farm.

In 1933 the School Board made the decision to bus all Carbon County eleventh and twelfth grades students to Price to finish high school. The Sunnyside school from then on was used only by students from first through tenth grades.

The Sunnyside school gym had a stage at the south end where plays and programs were presented. If the plays involved costumes, a classroom off the stage met the needs for this changing.

A row of metal racks and hooks between the classrooms on the west wing first floor provided a place to hang coats, hats, and put galoshes when students arrived at school in the wintertime.

In the 1940s, when the second boom in Sunnyside began, and the government' began subsidizing school lunches, the northeast Classroom on the ground floor became the food preparation room and the classroom next to it was where we ate our lunches. Some participated in the school lunch program and others continued bringing lunches from home or going home at noon.

The school was located a little over a half mile from our house and nearly one and a half miles from the last house in lower town. Every student and teacher in town walked to and from school.

On the south side of the school was a dirt playground. Ella Ruth remembers that in her elementary years the frame for the swing set didn't have swings and the children would swing hand over hand up the frame, across the top bar, and back down to the ground on the poles on the opposite end. She remembers there was no slide, then, too. But in my elementary years things had improved because I remember a swing set WITH swings, a slide and a horseshoe pitching pit.

East of the school, at the mouth of Hospital Canyon, was the ball field where we played softball, football and held May Day celebrations, complete with Maypole, to welcome spring's arrival. The mountain called Sunnyside Ledge was just across the road north of the school. During spring and fall, many school children played on this hill during recess and noon hours.

In 1945 the Dragerton school was completed and junior high students were bused to Dragerton for classes. A few years later the old Sunnyside school was abandoned and torn down, along with other buildings in town, because the No. 3 mine was expanding until it extended under Sunnyside, itself, making the town no longer safe to live in.

In the 1950s a new school, Peterson Elementary, was constructed on Edgehill Drive in Sunnydale. In 1959 a new high school, East Carbon High, was constructed below the Valley View addition of Sunnydale. Mother taught for many years at the Sunnyside School, Columbia Elementary and Peterson Elementary school. Her desire to help her students expand their horizons is well remembered, even today. She always had plays, musical programs and creative projects going in addition to seeing that every child learned the basics well. At the end of every school year in Sunnyside she took her students to the Indian writings up the canyon and then on to the rodeo grounds for games, contests and picnics. Her last day of school prognostications at every school delighted her students every year. Former students still say to me, "Mrs. Turner was the best teacher I ever had."

Some of my memories of the old Sunnyside school include the time dad, who was on the School Board and apparently tending me, took me, a pre-schooler, to Miss Justesen's first grade class for an hour while he met with her and other teachers. I wanted to come back the next day but she said, "You'll have to have another birthday first." I did go back the next year and had a great first grade experience.

I remember spending many evenings, winter and summer, playing games in the old gym. It was available to any group whenever school was not in session.

I learned to play horseshoes at the school playground under the tutorship of Boyd Lindsey who lived next door to the school. We had many great games, both singles and doubles.

Grant and I were janitors at the school for a year or two. We also had access to the shop in the basement and had a good time learning to use woodworking tools there.

My memories also take me back to when mother was teaching and she, Ella Ruth, Grant and I would sit together during the noon hour eating homemade whole-wheat bread sandwiches and each drinking a pint of milk in a fruit jar from home. Once in a while I'd trade with a classmate for his sandwich made of white bread. He'd have to throw in an apple and a piece of pie if I were to trade him today. Even then I'm not sure I'd make the trade.

The schools I attended while growing up in Sunnyside were great places to learn life's values and lessons. I wouldn't trade my early years with anyone. I just wish I could take my grandkids back there with me in reality instead of just in my memories.

The First School House (Photo courtesy GEA-HBLL-BYU)

School House (Photo courtesy Ernie Romero)

THE GYM

Some of my sons visited their old home recently and as I listened to their conversations, I realized that they were inviting some of their friends who still live in town to join with them in a basketball game. They would borrow the keys to the church recreation hall and try to find enough friends and relatives to make up two teams. They usually succeed. They do this each time they come home for a visit.

Gyms (or in this case recreation halls) play an important role in our lives, especially as we are growing up. In gyms we learn team work. They are also great places to participate in activities that release tensions. Each time my sons gather and head for the gym, I'm reminded of the early days in Sunnyside. The gym was the center of many community activities when I was growing up.

Churches didn't have recreation halls in the early days. Our Sunnyside church just had one large room, a relief society room behind the stage and two small classrooms in the west half of the basement. We gathered at the church for Mutual and/or Scout meeting, but after the meeting or, in some cases as part of it, we would end up at the gym in our old Sunnyside School and the fun games would begin. Often it wasn't basketball we played but a 1930s and 40s version of dodge ball. Here is how we played it:

The gym was regulation size, but not much more. On either side there was just enough room for a row of benches. During a regular basketball game, those watching kept their feet directly under their knees or under the benches. If a foot stuck out just a little there was always the danger of tripping one of the players.

At the north end of the gym was space for a row of

benches or chairs that was elevated about two feet. On the south end of the gym was the stage. Often there were no chairs or benches along the riser on the north. If chairs were there, we would take them to the other end, placing them on the stage. If left on the north riser, they would have been in the way of our dodge ball game.

This particular form of dodge ball had been played by my older brothers and their friends because I remember watching these older boys play the game and could hardly wait until I was old enough and big enough to play it. Three guys were chosen "It" and they got to go to the north end and try to dodge the missiles which were thrown at them. I call the thrown balls "missiles" because the dictionary describes a missile as "that which may be thrown or shot to do damage." And that describes the game we played to a T.

The missiles we used were any size balls that were available in the gym or adjoining supply room when we arrived. Usually we could count on about ten balls of various sizes from basketballs to volley balls.

The idea of the game was that all the guys who were not "It" lined up at half court and began launching balls (missiles) at those on the north end who were jumping and running back and forth trying to dodge them. The only rule was, "No hitting above the chest." When a launcher hit an "It," the two immediately changed places, the launcher then becoming an "It." The goal was to be "It" as long as possible.

When a ball was thrown and you were able to dodge it, it then bounced off the wall and back to the line of launching players. The balls were thrown with much gusto and zest and the turn-around time was instantaneous, or so it seemed. This was one of my favorite games. It took no skill, just instinct and luck. Some hits could leave a red spot right through your clothes.

When I played center field in baseball for Carbon College a few years later, I realized just where I got my good throwing arm. It was from those younger years when, at least twice a week, we were at the gym launching basketballs and volley balls just as hard as we could throw them. Coach Jewkes put me in center field because he said he liked the way I could throw from there to home plate and the ball only made one bounce before getting to the catcher.

As kids, we had open access to the gym whenever other events were not scheduled at the same time. Several of us would visit principal Harold Hansen at home and ask to borrow his school keys. I don't remember him ever saying no. When our gym activities were over and the balls put away, we returned his keys. No one ever mentioned adult supervision, and there was never any vandalism or destruction. We knew that if our behavior was appropriate we would always have access to the gym. Dad was on the school board and I know that he lobbied for this arrangement in all of the schools in the district.

Many other community activities took place in the school gym. The amusement hall was closed during most of these years and the gym was the only place big enough to hold these activities. Dances, wedding receptions, school productions, band concerts and many other events were held on a regular basis in that old gym. It was the community gathering place. The only one.

Many of the dances moved to the Dragerton School gym when that building was completed. Things changed then. There was more drinking and fighting. Officials were on hand to break up any fights before serious damage was done, but in the Sunnyside gym I don't ever remember even a serious argument. Times were changing and it wasn't necessarily for the better, at least as far as responsible behavior was concerned.

But in the days when the Sunnyside School gym was our only community center, children always attended wedding receptions along with their families, and the gifts the newly-weds received were always useful as well as appreciated. I remember once when dad bought a new, round galvanized tub, the kind we bathed in, and carried it, unwrapped of course, to the wedding reception of a newly married couple.

I seem to remember there was always homemade root beer with dry ice bubbling in it in five gallon milk cans which sat brewing in the foyer just east of the gym. And I remember everyone having a good time. After a short program, the dancing would begin. There were always plenty of refreshments; cake, cookies, candy, nuts and the ever-present root beer to hit the spot for this young attendee every time.

After the dances were moved to Dragerton, a few wedding receptions were still held in the Sunnyside School gym. Ardyth and I had our reception there when I was home on furlough from the Air Force in March 1952. I still remember the three sets of metal canisters we received as wedding gifts. Metal canisters have a long shelf life. We did, finally, use the second set. But the third set became rusty in a storage room before we got to use it and in the late 1970s I slipped it into the garbage without telling my wife. If I had told her my plans, we would still be saving it, in case we ever need it. We have other things we're saving that are older than that.

The following year, 1953, Ella Ruth and Jim had their wedding reception in the Sunnyside School gym, too. But the days of wedding receptions in that old gym were fast coming to a close.

In those early years, dances were held in the Sunnyside School gym often; during every holiday, special occasion and just for the joy of dancing. Some years it seemed like there was a dance every Saturday night. Music for the dances was provided by Jimmy Eaquinto and his accordion or various town orchestras. Dean and, later Ella Ruth, both played in these orchestras. The Anderson Brothers from Price provided most of the dance music in the last years of Sunnyside gym dances.

In 1958 when the new elementary and high schools in Sunnydale were completed, the Sunnyside School closed its doors for the last time. Another monument from my youth was gone.

As my sons returned home from the church gym, sweaty and laughing, I asked them how things went. They assured me that it was great fun and nice to see their old friends again. Good friendships never change and I hope that will always be so. I know that my friends and I had some great, never to be forgotten, character building experiences in the old Sunnyside gym.

HAIR

Hair styles are funny things. A few weeks ago my granddaughter came in with her hair looking like she had been swimming and just climbed out of the pool. She twirled happily around and said, "Gramps, look at my new permanent."

She called it a 'crunch' or a 'scrunch' or a 'crush' —or something like that. Whatever it was called it still looked like an unraveled rope that no amount of combing would ever untangle..

The following Sunday in church I watched a young man pass the Sacrament. He's a free-spirited kind of kid who has sported every haircut from bald to pony-tailed. This day his hair was cut so that it looked like someone had shaved his head but left just enough hair at the crown so it looked like he had on a skullcap. I had to look twice to make sure my eyes weren't fooling me.

We have a son with hair reaching to his shoulders. His mother has had many conversations with him about it, to no avail. He tells the story about one of his friends who got a haircut and lost 135 pounds. My wife asked how that could happen and my son answered, "He got his mother off his back."

I see lots of these kinds of hair styles among young people these days. I see lots of baggy clothes, unlaced sneakers, clothes with the labels on the outside and hightop boots on girls like we used to have to wear to work, too. I've watched styles come and go and come back again for more than half a century. Some of them go from one extreme to another but the one thing I don't see any more is girls with their hair in curlers or pincurls, covered by colorful bandannas.

In Sunnyside when I was growing up, Saturday seemed to be the day for hair washing and curling. Every female in town wanted to have clean, curly hair for church on Sunday.

Nearly all the little girls then sported Dutch-boy haircuts, bangs cut straight across their foreheads and the sides and back cut straight around just above their earlobes. They couldn't wait to grow old enough to get a permanent.

Perms in those days were accomplished by a machine that looked like it came straight out of a horror story. First the hair was rolled on metal rollers about the size of worn-down crayons. Then a pole with two-feet long electrical wires with metal clamps on the ends was rolled up to the chair and the beautician placed a clamp on each roller. They tell me that when this permanent machine was turned on to set the curls, it could really heat up the scalp. After what seemed like an eternity under that monster octopus, the clamps were undone, the rollers unrolled and tight little kinky curls, much like my granddaughter's hair, appeared. But no girl in those days left it like that. From then on, that newly-permed hair was rolled in curlers, set in finger-waves or pincurled to the desired style.

Sometimes curling irons were used but the early ones were not electrical and had to be heated on the stove. To use a blow dryer in those days, you simply sat on the back porch facing the wind or rode in the back of dad's truck.

In those long-gone days boys got haircuts whether they wanted them or not. And this was before electric clippers. Some boys got bowl-haircuts, where their parents literally put a bowl on their heads and clipped up to it. The 'skullcap' boy in church reminded me of these early bowl cuts.

But we had better than that. Mother was the one who operated our non-automatic clippers. She was a genius with the things. No wonder her hands later developed arthritis—the joints were probably worn out. Besides giving the girls Dutch-boy cuts, mother clipped six male heads of hair in her own family plus the heads of many other males who showed up regularly for haircuts at our house on the designated Saturdays.

Mother would squeeze the clipper handles as she moved smoothly up the backs of our necks and heads. This took skill, coordination and patience. She had all three. And she got the taper right every time. Once in awhile your hair would catch in the clippers and that would bring tears to your eyes. I believe mother could feel that pain. She was genuinely dismayed whenever that happened.

Dad cut my hair a few times when mother was out of town. If we ever go back to the old ways and have to use the hand clippers again and you have a choice, let your mother cut your hair. Dads lack cutting compassion.

When our nine children came along, I got involved in hair cutting as a matter of economics. By then electric clippers had arrived on the scene. My tapers in the back of their heads were more like steps. I mentioned to my wife in church recently, as I observed some of the teenage boys and their haircuts, that I was born forty years too soon. The boys had steps, ridges, initials and bare spots on their heads. And I'll bet they paid plenty for what I used to do for free.

We had one son who would wear a cap for ten days after each haircut until it was mostly grown out again. He would even wear the cap to bed. I maintain there's only a week between a good hair cut and a bad one, anyway. The more heads of hair I cut the more I appreciated what mother went through. And she didn't have electric clippers.

My brother Grant developed into a pretty good barber. He cut hair to earn a little extra money in his free time during his assignment in the Air Force. By the time he got out of the Service and back to college, he gave me and some of our classmates some pretty good trims. He even cut his own hair and it always looked great.

In the late 1940s electric hair clippers became available and Clayton Anderson started a barber shop in the bowling alley in Sunnydale. By then we all had jobs and could afford the fifty cent haircuts. One day we talked Clayton into taking a break and letting us boys cut each other's hair. We looked so bad that we all shaved our heads and spent the summer growing our hair back in time for school.

One payday I was getting a haircut from Clayton. I hadn't shaved for two days. At that age there wasn't much growth anyway, but I asked Clayton how much it would be for a haircut and a shave. With a twinkle in his eyes he said, "I'll give you the works for the same fifty cents." What a deal. I went for it.

When Ned Arambula came to town he not only took over our physical conditioning and scout leadership duties but he also gave haircuts to any boy who would sit still long enough. Mother could now hang up her clippers for good.

As my locks thin out with age, I can still see that old Sunnyside kitchen on haircutting Saturday afternoons. The haircuts began with dad and the older boys and worked down. We would sit on the stool under the sixty watt light globe, put the ready-to-be-washed dishtowel around our necks, pinning it in front with a safety pin and try to enjoy the next half hour with instructions to "hold still" or "turn your head this way."

Mother, wherever you are, if there is no electricity, I hope all the males are bald. You've already been through the hair cutting wilderness. You now deserve the promised land.

As my granddaughter left for home that day I said, "Your hair looks great. If I had more hair, I'd get mine looking like yours."

She turned with a grimace and retorted, "Ha! Ha! Gramps. You're real funny."

HAY

Moving up the freeway grade at nearly seventy miles per hour, the whipper-snapper passed me like I was standing still. How do these young drivers get away with that? And to add insult to injury, he had a load of hay. Not regular bales of hay, but the one-ton bales that look like they must be bound for Paul Bunyan's farm.

As I flashed my lights so he could move his rig over into the right lane, I wondered if that driver had ever lifted a bale of hay. I feel sorry for drivers and their new rigs today who are trying to get to the Promised Land without going through the wilderness. Eighteen-wheelers didn't always have that much power, and hay bales were not always that big. In fact, when I was a boy mechanical hay balers, like grams of fat, had not yet been discovered in my neck of the woods.

Below Sunnyside, where creeks and floods of past eras had left a flat area large enough to grow hay, and where mother and dad had lived in a tent when they were first married, Uncle Orson and other part-time farmers grew feed for their livestock. No sprinkling systems then! No sir. The water was diverted from the creek and coaxed down the rows, one row at a time. you could tell where the water did not make it to the end of the row by the dry or dead patches of stubble. If the snowpack was light or if Mother Nature did not release her water in the right amounts, much of the fields would appear dead or dying.

Floods were another story. These days a farmer counts his wealth in water shares. In earlier days the farmer had no wealth to count and faith was involved in putting bread on his table. I'm sure my vanishing freeway associate couldn't relate to any of this and maybe it's just as well.

The farmer of the 1930s needed access to a good team of horses, a hay mower if he was lucky enough to have one, a hay rake, and a good derrick in his stack yard. All farmers had pitchforks and hay wagons. For the most part these tools, with the possible exception of pitchforks, have vanished into history.

Since I witnessed their disappearance first hand, let me tell you about them. The farmer hitched up his team at daybreak to the metal-wheeled mower. The mower had cutting teeth that slid back and forth, mowing the hay. The teeth and blades extended out to the side of the mower about six feet. The turning wheels activated the blades and teeth. If a pheasant or skunk raised its head as the mower arrived, it remained headless for the rest of its natural life.

When the mowing was finished, the farmer returned to his equipment area, fed his team a little grain and hooked up the rake. The metal rake is the one most often seen today in old, rusting farm equipment piles. The rake tines were about four feet long and curved in a half circle. As he did with the mower, the farmer sat on a small metal seat in the middle of the unit, pushing and releasing pedals and the hand controls as needed. The reins were long enough to be tied together and looped around the farmer's neck. At the end of the field when turning was required, a good team would make the turn with very few commands. With an inexperienced team, however, the farmer had to pull on the reins and work to get the desired results. The rake piled the mown hay into rows.

Today, one farmer or contractor and one expensive piece of motorized equipment can do all of this in a few hours. It took the early farmer a few days to accomplish the same thing. Today, the farmer has the option of baling the hay, chopping it or cubbing it. Today, one man with his motorized loading and stacking equipment can bring the bales from the field, stack them in symmetrical, even rows and return home in time for dinner without putting on his gloves or touching a bale of hay. His one piece of motorized equipment may cost more than a farmer of the 1930s earned in a lifetime.

That early farmer then hitched his team to the hay wagon for the trip to the field. The wagon had a wooden platform about eight by twenty feet. A ladder at the front of the wagon permitted access to the top of the load. In the field, workers with pitchforks in hand would bring the forks full of hay to the wagon as it traveled between the rows of hay. We younger kids would tromp down the hay as it was placed on the wagon. Tolerating the sharp hay stems and breathing dusty hay leaves was not my idea of fun but we made the best of it by running and jumping as we compacted the hay, looking forward to the ride back to the stack yard when the wagon was fully loaded.

At the stack yard, we youngsters who were not big enough to handle a pitchfork, transferred our tromping to the haystack on the ground as the hay was removed from the wagon. The big, wooden log derrick and a good work horse were required to get the hay from the wagon to the stack. If you do much traveling in rural America, you may spot a rotting abandoned derrick. It looks like an unfinished log square with a large log or pole on an angle pointing upward. You may even be lucky enough to see one with the cable stretched between pulleys at the bottom and top of the pole. If you really get lucky you may see the hay fork with its rotting wood parts, rusting breakaway metal triangle frame and four or five metal tines about three feet long.

The derrick pole pointing skyward was attached to a cross member pole with a chain so that it could move in any direction. Here's how it worked: A cable ran from the fork, through the pulley at the top, down through the pulley at the bottom and hooked to the harness of the work horse. When the horse moved forward pulling on the cable, it pulled the fork full of hay up from the wagon. The direction the horse pulled would determine the direction of the pole and the fork full of hay. When the desired location on the haystack was reached, a worker would pull a rope attached to the fork, releasing the hay, which dropped onto the stack. A good worker would release the fork in the right spot to build an even haystack. A novice, or prankster, sometimes dropped a fork full of hay on one of the trampers. The dust, scratches and hay leaves in our eyes were occupational hazards and a good reason for wanting to grow up in a hurry.

One day I was assigned to lead the horse at the stack yard. I remember that day in great detail. The lead rope tied to the horse's halter was about three feet long. I was about the same size. When I began leading the horse with this short rope I was only a step or two in front of the horse. With the horse and its heavy load bearing down on me, I was sure that I would be stepped on. The more I tried to step faster than the horse to move out of his way, the faster the horse would move. The workers began yelling that I was going too fast. I explained my dilemma and they all laughed. It was no laughing matter. Backing the horse up was no problem, but moving forward brought fear and trembling to this six year old youngster. I was more than happy to work as a tromper on future loads.

Eventually, balers came into use and the pitchfork crews and trompers took their place in history. The first balers used wire and compressed the hay into very tight bales. Hooks about a foot long and resembling Disney's Captain Hook's replacement hand were then used to move the bales of hay around. Years later the baling wire was replaced by baling twine. Those same size bales today can be handled by a strong boy or man wearing a longsleeved shirt and a pair of gloves, lifting on the twine.

Call it a real find if in your travels you can spot a hay derrick AND a rusting pile of baling wire in an unused corner of an old farm operation.

With that eighteen-wheeler, hay carrying freeway driver now out of sight, I thought of my own hay experiences and wondered what his memories of hay will include.

HEROES

As I listen to my grandchildren talk about their heroes, too often they name names from the entertainment or sports world, people who give a good public 'show' but whose private lives are too often filled with anti-hero qualities. I'm saddened to think these are the people youngsters look up to in this day and age. When I compare these modern anti-heroes to the genuine, homespun heroes of my youth, I can see how broad the gap is between those days and now.

There was no TV when I was a boy and we spent very little time listening to the one radio we had. Our heroes then lived right in town and were our family members, neighbors and townsfolk. Sunnyside was full of heroes in my young eyes.

There was Buster Preston who was Santa Claus for as long as I can remember. And there was The Lindsey Brothers Basketball Team. They were all great guys. Boyd taught me how to play horseshoes when I was still in grade school, a game I enjoy to this day.

Then there was Harold Hansen, the school principal, who handed us the keys to the gym whenever several of us wanted to play basketball or other games there. It may have helped that dad was on the school board but I don't think that was the reason because he let other kids use the gym, too. We didn't require supervision to use the gym because we had all learned how we were expected to act at home. There was never any vandalism. We didn't even know the word in those days.

Some of my own peer heroes were the Nitsuma boys, Henry and the twins, Harry and Harold. They were my horseshoe playing partners and horse riding buddies. They took more than their share of flak when Pearl Harbor was bombed but, somehow, survived that sad period in our town's history. Their father was killed in the terrible mine accident in 1945. They were my quiet heroes.

And I'll never forget Horace Naylor who let two youngsters enjoy the thrill of watching him work the hoist house machinery when we were much too young to be anywhere near the mine. And there was Bob Heers, the mine superintendent, who helped a group of would-be skiers build a ski slope and rope tow.

And everyone liked Jimmy Eaquinto and his accordion. If there was music, Jimmy was nearby. And speaking of music, I'll never forget Harold Hansen's wife, Ruby, who taught us younger family members piano lessons and could play so beautifully herself although the middle finger on her hand had been amputated.

I'll never forget Mike Fratto, a big, strong, burly guy who was gentle with young kids. We didn't have 4th of July money of our own so he often shared with us kids the firecrackers he had bought with his own hard-earned money.

Max Ledger was another hero to me. He would bring his football and organize our games on the main street in town. I played receiver and I know from experience that Max could throw the football a mile or more.

My Sunnyside heroes didn't have extraordinary talents or fame, or make huge sums of money. They were just good people we enjoyed being around. People like Avonna Blackburn who could bring tears of patriotism every time she sang "God Bless America." And Frank Campagni, who could make his saxophone sing and was fun to be around. And I'll never forget my cousin Phillip Turner. When he came back from the war, he helped us young kids make specially constructed rubber guns and even joined in our 'shoot-em-up' rubber gun games. He also did great repair work on cars, charging much less than we would have had to pay elsewhere.

Then there were guys like John Preston, the father of my friend Johnny, who could make his fiddle dance and kept working and supporting his family even after his leg had to be amputated. And I'll never forget Bones Watkins who made Christmas a little brighter by placing his lighted Christmas tree on the roof of his apartment above the hospital. This was long before outdoor Christmas decorations.

And then there were Mac McKinley and Ned Arambula who became scoutmasters for a group of active, fun-loving young boys. And Ellis Peacock, the store butcher, who was always there with a smile and a piece of candy for us.

Our schools were full of heroes. Galen Wycherly was the great fifth grade teacher who, with a smile, welcomed kids into his home on weekends when we kids didn't have any idea that he might have wanted a little personal time of his own. Lee and Royal Allred and their wives were all teachers and great to be around whether in school or out. My own mother was one of the greatest teachers who ever lived, even while raising a large family, supporting dad in all his activities, and taking in grandchildren when their mother died. I still have people who, when they find out who I am, say, "Your mother was the best teacher I ever knew. I'll never forget her."

Then there were guys like Leon Pressett who spent time with younger team members showing them how to improve their basketball skills. He invited me to play in the first annual tournament in Helper, sponsored by one of the service clubs. This tournament is still being held annually almost fifty years later. Leon was two years older than me but never made fun of me or treated me like a nuisance.

Our family was full of heroes including my dad who spent his spare time in community service. I believe he held every volunteer job in town at one time or another. And he had a fun sense of humor. My brothers and sisters took the time to teach me riding, athletic and social skills that I value to this day.

When I entered my teens I came in contact with Gus Burdis and his brother, Frank, who ran the bowling alley. They were great heroes. When we teenagers needed a place to dance, Gus would let us move the fixtures around at the bowling alley and we had plenty of space for our dance or party.

Besides my sisters, the other older girls in town were also great sports and fun to be around even though little brothers can sometimes be a pain in the neck. Some of the older girls I remember fondly are the Gilligan sisters, Ruth Preston, Vera Nuzio, June McFarland, Pauline Roseman, the Naylor girls, Yvonne Della Corte and the Eaquinto sisters.

When Sunnydale came into existence my hero list expanded with people like the Murphys, Jerry Hernandez, Jimmy Howa, C.P. Greenwell and a host of others like barber, Clayton Anderson, and more.

And who will ever forget Andy Anderson and his family when they pulled into town from southern California in that old 'Whippet' car loaded with their belongings. Andy and his wife taught both school and entrepreneurship. He provided his son Robert, and some of the rest of us, with a good job checking coats and hats at the Saturday night dances in the Dragerton school gym. In addition to the dimes and quarters we charged, we often got good tips from some of the tipsy partygoers and had a ringside seat for the occasional brawl that broke out. Andy was like our dad when it came to finding extra work for their children.

The young married couples in town were great examples for a young lad who benefitted from being exposed early to their examples. There were our cousins Wade and Catherine Turner, Tug and Lula Morley who hired Grant and me to be the first baby sitters for their children when they went dancing, the Andrews, the Prestons (all of them), my brother Dean and his wife Pauline, and a number of others.

I'll never forget the Anderson twins from Price who furnished the orchestra for many of our dances. As a small boy I often sat through the dance visiting with Gerald Anderson who played the drums, and Derald who played the trombone, and entertained with special numbers on his musical saw.

Other heroes who come to mind include the Pattersons, Pressetts, Dennisons, all the Jones families, the Pederivas who always had candy kisses to share with us kids, the Peacocks, the Durrants and numerous others. A trip to Menotti's store below town exposed me to more great people. I'll never forget Albert, Freddie and their beautiful sister Elsie. Sunnyside Junction gave us the Flemetis family with their warm smiles and friendly attitudes. The list is endless.

Sunnyside and it's environs was full of heroes, both male and female. And they included everyone from the mine superintendent through all social, ethnic, religious and economic levels. Everyone knew everyone else and cared about them. When a beef or pig was butchered, many families benefitted, some not even knowing who had placed the piece of meat on their kitchen tables.

Those were great days. A greeting, a handshake, a hug, and a welcoming smile. I don't seem to see as much of that anymore. I wish my grandkids had real heroes. The kind I grew up with.

HORSES AND MULES

When dad took over the company corral and barn in 1932, horses and mules, along with various other critters became part of our lives. A canyon breeze blowing north through the barnyard was a constant reminder to us, and the nearby neighbors, how lucky we were that dad had steady work. So we got used to the pungent odors carried along by the breeze.

Our livestock experiences are among my favorite memories. One of dad's jobs was to shoe the company horses and mules. He became an expert at this task. The horseshoe shop was located at the edge of the creek bank in front of our house. It was here that dad and the mules got better acquainted. You, who have not had much experience with mules, need to understand that mules are some of the most stubborn animals on earth. But these company mules were no match for my dad. My earliest recollection of that horseshoe shop was when, at a very young age, I wandered in and witnessed first hand dad and a mule trying to outsmart each other.

Dad had tied a rope from the mule's neck to its lower back leg, around its neck again and back to the other hind leg which was raised and ready for a new shoe. When I arrived, dad had a rasp in hand and was swinging it at the mule as he quoted scriptures. The mule, kicking and braying, was answering back. I was quickly hustled out of the shop, but I know that dad had the last word.

Some of the animals I still remember were: Abe, a big work horse that pulled a dump wagon at the coke ovens; Nellie, a gentle mule that pulled carts in the mine. She was our favorite riding mule. Monk, another big work horse that was sold soon after we arrived. There were a couple of other mules but they weren't docile enough to make friends with. Grant and I rode Abe and Nellie around town before we got our own riding horses.

Our family owned a mare, Babe, a gentle, sweet horse who foaled Bolly, a feisty, frisky, colt. Big brother Dean broke and raised Bolly until he moved away.

As the years went by, Bolly became a fat, perverse, lazy horse that would rear up when he didn't want to be ridden. Dad was working at the tipple across the creek one day and looked toward home just as I climbed on Bolly for a ride. Bolly reared up and I slid off. Dad came running across the footbridge. As he passed the scrap iron pile by our house, he picked up a threefoot length of pipe. He took the reins from me and jumped on Bolly's back. As Bolly began to rear up again, dad hit him on the side of the neck. The hit stunned Bolly for a minute, but this horse was smart enough to get the message the first time. Dad told me to climb back on and go riding. He returned to his work at the tipple. Bolly did not rear up any more that day.

As Grant and I got older, dad bought us our own horses. He bought a small palomino mare from Tubby Jones. She was called Queenie and was just right for me. Dad also purchased The Brown Mare from Milt Thayne in Wellington. This was Grant's horse. The Brown Mare was a spirited, fast horse. We were now ready to compete in friendly racing with the other boys in town, and Grant was the ideal jockey. With our slow mine horses and mules we had been only spectators at races in the past, but that all changed when we got our own mounts.

We rented out the horses and mules for 25¢ per hour. With Bolly not wanting to leave the barn, a rider on another horse had to take the reins and lead Bolly. On the return trip to the barn, Bolly's rider could now take the reins and ride like the other riders back toward the barn. Bolly lived for over twenty years.

We bought Old Dick from Uncle Orson. This old steed had 'ringbones' in his front feet. He was a good old slow, gentle rental and a good deer hunting pack horse. Our horses wintered in Pasture Canyon above town. One spring all of the horses returned but Old Dick. A year or two later I found his remains in a small ravine in the canyon. It appeared that he had rolled onto his back, sliding into the narrow ravine and couldn't get back out.

Our last equine purchase was Tony. This old roan horse was gentle and another good rental and pack horse. Dad bought him for $20. On one deer hunting trip, old Tony got stuck between two trees. Tony was about three feet wide, but with panniers (pack saddles) on he was about two feet wider on each side. Tony could normally walk between trees that were four feet apart, but when he tried it with the panniers on, he came up short. Struggling to get between the trees, and frustrated that he couldn't, he lunged forward and became stuck. We spent an hour removing his load and getting Tony unstuck before we were back on the trail again.

On the same deer hunting trip, with Grant on The Brown Mare, we started down a steep hillside, pausing to let the horses eat some grass along the way. Grant's saddle cinch was not tight enough. When his horse started eating with its head down near its front legs, facing downhill, Grant and the saddle started sliding forward. Grant rolled to the ground as his saddle passed over the horse's head and front legs. The horse stayed calm. We all had a good laugh as Grant replaced his saddle, cinched it tighter, and continued down the trail.

We were not allowed to ride horses on Sunday. Sunday was the Lord's day. When the new mine superintendent, William Walker, moved to Sunnyside, his son had a horse that was housed in our corral. Superintendent Walker asked dad if one of our boys could go riding with his son for the boy's first ride in the new town this next Sunday. Dad indicated that they could go riding after church. Grant was appointed the Sunday rider. While they were riding, Grant explained to the new boy, Billy Neff Walker, our family Sunday riding rules. We went on many rides with Billy and his horse, Paint, from then on, but they were done the other six days of the week.

My experiences with horses were all positive. If there horses in heaven I'd like to do some more riding. One thing I am sure of. At least dad won't end up shoeing any more ornery mules.

The author and brother Grant with Nellie, the Mine Mule (Photo author's collection)

Jake Vogrinic 1927 (Photo courtesy Mildred Babcock)

ICE

My granddaughters were helping my wife get the table ready for the Sunday gathering. It was wintertime. The girls were putting ice cubes in the glasses they were setting on the table. As I wandered into the kitchen I quipped, "Why are you kids wasting ice cubes? It's winter."

Ignoring me, they continued their tasks and I again spoke great words of wisdom that went nowhere.

I can remember the early days when ice was almost not a renewable resource. If you had any you were lucky, except during the winter when you didn't need it and it was outside everywhere.

We had no fridge or freezer. When cold weather set in, if someone killed a cow the beef was divided among the neighbors. Our quarter of beef hung under the eaves on the north side of the house. It came down and a piece was cut off when mother planned to cook a roast. Then the remains were re-wrapped in the clean white flour sack again and re-hung. Very soon, before it went bad, what was left of the meat was cut, cooked and shredded and mother bottled it, borrowing someone's pressure cooker to safely seal the bottles. This bottled meat was used in soups and stews in the summer.

In the 1920s and 30s, blocks of ice began to be delivered to Sunnyside and a few lucky families bought an ice box. This wooden ice box was about three and a half feet high, two feet wide and one foot deep. The top was hinged and under this lid there was a compartment which held a block of ice. Food to be cooled was placed in the lower, slightly larger compartment. This complete unit was insulated and a block of ice would usually last one day. The melting ice drained into a drip pan in the bottom of the ice box. This pan needed to be emptied two or three times a day.

Although we didn't have an ice box in Sunnyside originally, we did have one for a couple of years when we lived in Provo in 1939 and 1940. Ice boxes were eventually replaced by electric refrigerators.

In those early years in Sunnyside we had a hand-cranked ice cream freezer that could hold about two gallons of ice cream. It must have been the only ice cream freezer in town because everyone came to borrow it. I don't remember hearing, "Can we borrow YOUR freezer?" It was always, "I came to get the big green freezer." I didn't realize it was OURS for years.

In the winter we gathered ice to make ice cream from a variety of buckets and troughs outside. In the summers we bought ice from the ice house. The blocks of ice were placed in a number three round, metal tub and then broken into smaller chucks with an axe. It was now ready to place in the wooden freezer barrel in which was set the metal inner bucket containing the ice cream ingredients mother had mixed together. After everyone took turns cranking the freezer handle, with salt and chunks of ice steadily added to the outer barrel to keep it cold, the ice cream was ready to eat. Those of us who remember that ice cream know that there has never been any ice cream since to equal the rich, creamy taste of that homemade ice cream.

The ice house was located by the railroad tracks just north and east of the bridge across from our house. It was mostly underground and much like the potato cellars you see in many farmyards in rural America.

During the winter the train would arrive with one boxcar loaded with large blocks of ice about one third to one half the size of a modern washer or dryer. The blocks of ice were about eighteen inches thick. The train would pull the ice car in front of the ice house. Then a ramp of boards was placed from the door of the boxcar to the door of the ice house. More boards were angled inside to the back wall of the ice house. The blocks of ice were slid out the door, down the ramp and to the back of the room where the worker there, using large metal hooks, piled them onto each other. The ice was stored in sawdust which helped keep it frozen. The blocks of ice were then sold to customers throughout the summer.

As a youngster, I visited the ice house in Provo. It was in a building on the same level as the boxcar filled with ice. Workers placed metal strips on the railroad dock and a gentle push moved the block of ice from the boxcar to the storage unit. The unit temperature was controlled by a compressor and the freezer did not need sawdust to keep it cool. Being a city, Provo had all the latest inventions.

Back in Sunnyside, ice for drinks at the confectionery started as large chunks at the ice house. They were broken into smaller pieces and stored in a cooler behind the counter. My friend Martin Rodosh's job at the confectionery was to hammer the blocks into smaller sizes that fit into a wooden bucket. With a sharp ice pick he would then work the ice into chips ready for fountain drinks. Once in awhile slivers from the wooden bucket would float to the top of a drink.

Many years later when, as a father myself, we built a new Drive Inn and Malt Shop, and were reviewing equipment needs, the supplier asked if we wanted an ice machine that would make cubes, chips, crushed, round, or half-round pieces? Now, instead of just ice, we had many options.

Eventually refrigerators replaced ice boxes, the beef came out from under the eaves, ice cubes were available in every home and homemade ice cream was easier to make any time of the year. With the new electric ice cream makers, another family work project passed into history. And with

Baskin-Robbins thirty one flavors, vanilla ice cream ONLY became a thing of the past.

Another part of the ice history in Sunnyside involved the ever useful DRY ICE.

Dry ice is made by processing and compressing carbon dioxide into solid form. A dry ice plant was located in Wellington in the early days. Dry ice was unique to us because it did not leave a wet spot when it melted, and it put the fizz in homemade root beer. But we learned it would burn our hand if left in one spot very long.

At social events at the Sunnyside School gym or church, five gallon cans were on hand for the drinks. A small bottle of root beer extract was placed in each can, three pounds of sugar and water to fill the can were added, stirred and mixed, then chunks of dry ice were placed in the cans and the mixture really started fizzing. White fumes drifted out of the cans and in a few minutes the best root beer available anywhere would be consumed by all present. Homemade root beer is another of those historical events you can learn about only by visiting with grandma or grandpa.

At the present time, fridges and freezers are cooled by freon. Since freon has been associated with depleting the ozone layer, we may have to give it up for something, perhaps, more costly and less desirable. If certain anti-technology zealots have their way, some modern inventions may pass into history as ice boxes have done. We may be back to cutting chunks of ice out of the river and hanging a side of beef under the eaves again. But then again, if mad cow disease spreads across the world, we may have to give up beef also.

I happened into the kitchen again as my granddaughters were finishing up with the water portion of the meal preparations. One of them piped up, "Gramps, when are you going to get a good fridge, like ours, so we can put the ice and cold water into the glasses at the same time just by pressing a button on the front? It would save us a lot of time."

I'm not sure that in the future this generation will have anything remotely resembling the good old days. But then again, hasn't every generation enjoyed the good old days once they passed into history?

JOBS

In an effort to keep myself and a couple of sons busy during our slow season we started a new business. My wife would have none of it. She said that at age sixty-five I should be slowing down, not looking for new experiences. I reminded her that at age sixty-five I don't have that much time left so I have to move a little faster to get it all done. She walked away shaking her head.

We came upon this new business quite by accident. I wanted some curbing around the yard and shrubs. I called the guy listed in the phone book who does this. He said I'll call you in thirty days. That was over a year ago. Rather than wait for his call, we checked into the equipment, etc. and $15,000 later we're into the curbing business and can't keep up with the requests.

In business I've learned that if you emphasize quality and a good relationship with the customer, you don't have to worry about competition. There isn't any! I observed that in dad and his part-time business dealings. If the customer had a problem, he got the product free. I was with dad when he gave away quarts of milk, bushels of peaches and apples, and spent many hours in community service. Dad was always looking for ways to fill a need or solve a problem—the two characteristics of a good salesman.

When I was growing up in Sunnyside money was scarce. If you wanted some, you found a job. Grant and I were probably the first male babysitters, for pay, in Sunnyside as we tended for the Morleys on Saturday nights as they went dancing.

When we were old enough we delivered eggs, milk and chickens. Then came newspapers. We scoured the highway between Price and Sunnyside many times collecting return-able pop and beer bottles. We also fed chickens, pigs, cows and horses although no money changed hands for these chores.

And speaking of beer bottles, during World War II, three bunk houses were built in Sunnyside to house the additional coal miners needed in the war effort. Some of these miners drank beer. Some drank it by the quart. Some gave young boys a monetary tip when they had finished with a quart of beer and the boys were delivering newspapers and gathering up empty beer bottles at the bunk houses. I was one of those boys.

We also gathered up scrap iron and copper. It was taken to Price when we had a truckload and sold to the scrap dealer there.

Because dad was barn manager and we had horses, both our own and some company horses and mules, and lots of Sunnyside kids liked to ride horses but didn't have their own, but did have money, we put it all together and started renting out the horses and mules at twenty-five cents per hour. This was a real bargain for everyone. We did not always have enough horses for everyone who showed up with their quar-ters. On the other hand, on slow days our customers got fifty cents worth of riding for a quarter.

Grant and I sold Christmas trees, too, for three or four years. Getting the trees was wet, hard work and our cus-tomers got a bargain when I compare our trees to the ones sold these days.

During some of the summers of my youth, we spent part of them in Provo at our new home. Our neighbor was Ariel Ballif, a professor at B.Y.U. His son, Jae, is my age and we were good friends. Through his father, when a track meet or other athletic event was held in the old stadium, we got jobs selling food and drinks in the stands. We got to see some great track meets and earn a little money at the same time. During these summers in Provo, we also worked on farms in Orem picking fruit and berries. One summer I worked as a custodian at B.Y.U. when nearly all the classes and buildings were on lower campus.

As we got older we began advancing toward full-time jobs. My first part-time/full-time job was as a custodian at the Sunnyside School. The old desks were mounted four in a row, hooked together at the bottom by two 4-by-10 slats. We would slide the rows of desks to one side of the room, dust mop or sweep the floor, move the rows to the other side of the room, sweep again, then place them back where they started out. The floor got a lot of wear.

The summer I was fifteen years old, dad got Grant and me a job at the coke ovens. I break out in a sweat just thinking about this hardest job ever. It was a learning experience, however, because no job since then has been too difficult.

The summer following the coke ovens job, Grant and I got work at the asphalt. When we went to the quarry, it was almost like a Boy Scout camp in a war zone. It was hard work, great fun, and we got paid well.

By this time we were back in Sunnyside to stay, so I finished my high school experience as a senior in Price. The new service station in Sunnydale was ready to open and I was hired to work there. I worked after school, on Saturdays, and during the summers.

While attending Carbon Junior College, I was hired to work for the Utah Fuel Company. I was assigned to the tipple as a "boney picker." The skills and equipment required were: hard-toed shoes, hard hat, lunch bucket, quick hands, and good eyes. This was my first year-round, eight-hour job, but at age nineteen it was about time.

This job consisted of picking the rocks (boney) from the coal as it slid down the shakers toward the crushers. There were four of us, two on each side of the shakers. The pay was good and I worked from 3:30 p.m. to 10:30 p.m. My last class in Price ended at 2 p.m. We rode home, changed into work clothes and punched in at 3:30 p.m.

My friend Jim Murphy and I rode home from Price together. He had a job at the store and also reported for work at 3:30 p.m. My job lasted several months and then I got serious about dating.

I was dating Ardyth and when we got serious about steady dating, I would visit her after work almost every night. Dad was finding it harder and harder to wake me up in the mornings in time to drive to college in Price. Because of my long hours, my eyes began twitching and I began to have spasms in my back muscles. Mother suggested that I visit the doctor.

The doctor asked about my schedule. Up at 7 a.m., school from 8:30 a.m. to 2 p.m., work from 3:30 p.m. to 10:30 p.m., date at 11 p.m. and to bed at 1 a.m. He shook his head and said that I'd have to give up something because I needed more sleep. I gave up full-time work.

After visiting with Jim Murphy and both our supervisors, Jim and I changed jobs. At the store I got off at 6:30 p.m. and my dating started about 8 p.m. When I returned their daughter by 10 or 11 p.m., both Gibson parents were all smiles and our relationship improved.

After a few months at the store, the manager at the service station asked if I'd like to come back to work for him. We made the change and I worked at the station until graduation from Carbon Junior College and my enlistment in the Air Force in June, 1951.

This same June was the end of my Sunnyside work days

and also the end of my days living in Sunnyside. When I returned to civilian life, married, four years later my parents had moved to Dragerton, and old Sunnyside, as I had known it, was disappearing fast.

My father taught me to understand economics. If you wanted money jingling in your pockets, you worked for it. The money we earned by gathering pop and beer bottles did not pay for the gas as he drove us along that highway between Sunnyside and Price, but we were learning about earning our own money. And that's the way dad wanted it. We learned a lot of good lessons growing up in Sunnyside.

LANGUAGE

In the 1930s and 40s in Sunnyside I was in awe of some of my friends. They spoke the same English we all spoke when playing and learning together yet, in their homes, they spoke fluently with their parents the language of the "old country" from which their parents had come. Sometimes I listened to Greek, sometimes Italian, sometimes Japanese, sometimes Spanish and sometimes one of the Slavic languages. Although I didn't understand a word at these times, my friends could jump from the language spoken at home to English and back again without missing a beat.

Until recent years I thought my "reading, writin' and 'rithmatic" days were over but I'm finding that in this day and age I'm having to learn a whole new language just to stay conversant in English. Some modern terms would have had an entirely different meaning when I was growing up in Sunnyside. For example:

MICROWAVE would have been what girls did to their hair with bobby pins, waving lotion and smaller finger crimps.

INTERNET was where you wanted to land the fish on your hook.

CHILD'S BEEPER was the noise a tricycle rider made just before he ran into you.

BUNGEE CORD would have been the notes a piano player hit when playing classical music.

ANOREXIC would have been the wife of Uncle Orexic.

RECYCLED was going back over the same route with your bicycle.

HAIR GEL was what you got in your jello if the waitress didn't wear the required by law hair net.

OLESTRA would have been the new Italian family who just moved into town.

SATELLITE DISH would have been what you brought the potato salad in to the picnic.

HEAVY METAL was when it took two guys to load a piece of scrap iron onto the back of the truck.

ROCK AND ROLL was what happened to grandpa when he got too close to the edge of the porch in his rocking chair.

POLITICAL ACTION was voting the straight Democratic ticket or being silent about it if you voted any other way.

RED NECK happened when you did not wear a hat while spending the day out in the sun.

SEXUAL HARASSMENT would have been when your big sister hit you and mother wouldn't allow you to hit her back.

SINGLE PARENT was when dad went to the ball game and mother attended the PTA Meeting.

GAY COMMUNITY was Sunnyside on Christmas Day or the 4th of July.

DRIVE BY SHOOTING was when the farmer got his deer while on his way out to his field.

POLICE ACTION was when a deputy helped direct parking at a football game in Price.

DRUGS were what the doctor gave you when you were really sick.

UNDERAGE SMOKING happened to little kids when they stood too near the fire at the weiner roast.

RAP MUSIC was what we did to our music books before going out in the rain.

AFFIRMATIVE ACTION was what dad took when he found out you had misbehaved in school.

BANKRUPTCY would have been the term used to describe a banker with a ruptured appendix.

PIZZA was the name of the band teacher.

JOGGING STROLLER was what you were after walking around town with your friends and you realized you were late for supper.

COUCH POTATO was when you were at a party and your potato rolled off your plate and lodged in the space between the arm and frame of the couch you were sitting on.

TANNING SPRAY would have been what you did when you got a spanking you thought would never end.

LAW SUIT was how a judge dressed.

BOY'S EAR RING was something that happened to your ear if you stood too close to an exploding firecracker.

DIET was something 'floozies' did to make their hair bright red.

BUSTED was what you did to the shell of a hard boiled egg before you could eat it.

GANG was what we called the crew working on the railroad.

SMOKING POT was what you had on the stove if you got distracted while cooking supper.

CALL WAITING was what you did after you told Operator Number Four who you were so she could connect you to the person who had called for you earlier.

E MAIL came right after the postmaster put the last letter for Durrant in the box.

WONDERBRA was what adolescent girls had to decide about buying before too much longer.

WEB PAGE was how the old catalog looked after hanging in the outhouse for awhile.

MOUNTAIN BIKE was any bike you rode above the 6,000 feet level.

V-CHIP was what a kid got in his tooth when the guy behind pushed his head at the drinking fountain.

SNOWBOARD was what you carried in from the wood-pile in the wintertime.

SPRAY ON was what you got if you surprised a skunk while thinning beets.

RANGE ROVER was what you did in the spring while trying to find all the horses that had been taken up to pasture in the canyon over the winter.

LIPOSUCTION would have been how a returning G.I. described kissing in France when the Allies liberated that country.

DOWNLOADING was the angle you parked your truck to make it easier for shoveling coal into the back of it.

FAT GRAMS was what we called one of the Graham's overweight kids.

WINDSURFING would have been a hoped for tailwind while ice skating.

FLAGGER was the student who got to raise the flag at the beginning of the school day.

"GIVE ME FIVE" was what a housewife, planning to bottle fruit, said to dad in the fall when he drove into town from a trip to Utah County with a truckload of bushels of fruit.

HOOKER was what one fisherman yelled to another when he saw a splash in the water.

WEED was what we pulled when they got too thick or too high.

SHOOT UP was what we did to a bulls-eye target with our rifle the week before the deer hunt.

SPEED was what the officer said you were doing as he wrote out the ticket.

DOPE was a term used for someone who did something stupid.

TRIP was when we went to Price.

FAR OUT was when we continued on to Provo.

HOMEBOY was noted by your name on the absentee list sent to the principal's office.

PROTEST was something you did when the food was going around the table but they wouldn't pass it to you.

WASTED was food that spoiled because preservatives were unheard of.

FREE RADICAL was a guy just finishing his shift on the picket line during a mine strike.

PUMPING IRON would have described a train going up a steep grade.

COMPUTER was what you did in your head during an arithmetic test.

I've learned other new words since my early days in Sunnyside and I fear, if the trend continues, I'll learn many more before I'm through. When I think about it, maybe the languages my youthful friends used at home and the languages my grandchildren speak won't be so far apart after all.

NEWS

There were five sources for news in the 1930s and 40s in Sunnyside. Between all five you could crunch the words and meanings and stay current on most local happenings.

The five sources were: (1) The telephone. There were three public phones and they were all party lines. (2) The radio. There was only one radio per family in those days and it sat in a prominent spot in the living room. (3) The postmaster. It didn't matter that the postmaster was female. She was still called the postmaster. (4) My dad. (5) The Sunnyside column in the Sun Advocate, the weekly newspaper from Price.

We didn't need the ten o'clock news or CNN in those days. Sunnyside was our world. If it didn't happen to someone in town it probably wasn't newsworthy. Old timer's disease sometimes hampers my memories but some recollections never leave. The news sources I remember so well didn't bother with gossip, but facts. Just the facts, ma'am.

We had one of the three public phones in town. The phone was about the size of a small breadbox and hung on the wall. you spoke into a little round unit about the size of a small aerosol lid that stuck out from the box about six inches. At the top of the box were two black beehive shaped bells. The listening piece that you held up to your ear was about the size of a drinking glass. A wire chord went from the earpiece to the phone. The chord was about two feet long. On the side of the box, opposite the earpiece was the winder, or ringer, that would ring the bells. It had a handle similar to the old manual pencil sharpeners and you would wind this to make the bells ring.

Our number was two longs followed by two shorts. This

was the length of the rings. Forget about phone books. You could list all of the available numbers on a post card and still have room for a message and address.

When our number was rung, only the grown-ups were supposed to answer the phone. The little kids couldn't reach the phone without a stool anyway since it was five feet up on the wall. Modern answering devices had nothing on us. Whoever answered the phone had to say, "Sunnyside Central." If your voice hadn't changed yet, the operator on the other end would say, "Please go get your mother or dad."

If the call was not for someone in our family the operator would say, "Mr. So and so is on the line for Mr. Such and Such. Go get him and have him call Operator Four." Not only were phones in short supply, but I don't remember any operator with a higher number than Eight.

In the early days I was too small to answer the phone but was never too small to run up or down town and get the person asked for. Our phone was in the kitchen. I can't prove this but I believe dad had it installed there so we would have plenty of chairs for everyone who wanted to listen in on the phone conversation.

Sometimes when we notified the persons wanted on the phone, their family members would also join them. A phone call to our phone often included a kitchen full of visiting friends, relatives and neighbors, making it difficult for the person on the phone to hear the other end of the conversation.

In small towns in those days a tragedy in one family included pain for everyone. Happy events for anyone were also shared with the entire town.

Party lines meant that all phones used common lines. If someone else was using one of the other phones, no problem, just lift the receiver and listen in. And you knew when someone was on the line because every ring that was cranked was heard on the other phones as well as your own. All for one and one for all. To get an operator you just lifted the receiver, cranked the ringer about three turns for a long ring and the next voice would be that of the operator.

During my growing years we moved to Provo and back to Sunnyside two different times. Our first phone in Provo was nothing like the ones in Sunnyside. It was black and sat on a table. It had one line. The speaker and receiver were on one hand-held unit which sat on a cradle-stand. We also had a phone book. The operator said, "Number please?" the minute you picked up the phone and it only rang in the house you were calling. Our first number there was 309R. Later it was 1676W, and still later a dial was added and you did your own dialing. Numbers now contained two letters and five numbers. Finally, phones evolved to the seven digit numbers we have at the present time.

So much for early phones. Our news came via the party line or listening to a one-sided phone conversation in our kitchen.

The radio was our next source of news. It brought us county, state and national news once a day but it had more action programs than news. Programs such as "The Lone Ranger," "The Shadow," "Superman," "Amos and Andy," "Burns and Allen" and "Major Bowes Amateur Hour." We all remember Sunday evening October 30, 1937 when Orson Welles broadcast his "War of the Worlds." I remember dad, during the program, worriedly walking out on the porch and looking searchingly into the skies. He wasn't the only one across the country who did this, either. When asked about it later, he said he just went out for a breath of fresh air. We smiled at his answer.

The postmaster was our neighbor and a good source of

the latest news. She would come in our back door a couple of times a week and sit at the kitchen table to visit. Since everyone picked up their mail at the post office and had time to stop and visit, Mrs. Jones knew all the latest news. She never gave advice or passed judgement, she simply related the news. Mother was a school teacher in addition to raising her seven children. When she was home she was always busy baking, cooking, sewing, ironing, cleaning or preparing lessons in the kitchen. She was a great listener. We always got first hand, up to date news from Mrs. Jones.

Dad also knew what was happening in town. He worked at the tipple weighing coal cars, was a member of the Union Board, member of the School Board, member of the Town Council, and member of our LDS Ward Bishopric. If he and Mrs. Jones were in the kitchen at the same time, you couldn't get a word in edgewise.

The Sun Advocate was always a good source for local, as well as county, news. These community news columns in existing weekly newspapers remain much the same today as they were all those years ago.

The sad news was when young local soldiers, sailors and marines serving in World War II were reported wounded, missing or killed in action. Mine cave-ins, deaths or accidents touched the lives of all of us.

Happy news events were weddings, announcements of new babies, dances, programs, school events, Christmas and Fourth of July celebrations and activities, and the end of the war.

We picked up all the news around our kitchen table. There were times when the news was definitely slanted toward the Democratic persuasion since all the families in town, and nearby, were Democrats. But one thing about it, we did not have to change channels because of commercials.

More of my time today is spent listening to, watching and reading the news but, somehow, I feel less informed. Is that possible?

Sunnyside news was first-hand, current and interesting. And, it was always G rated. I really miss our old news sources.

Nine Mile To Whitmore: A Canyon Odyssey

This summer we had our family reunion in Nine-Mile Canyon. This canyon is famous for its Indian Writings and other historical features including the ranch of the famous early cattle baron, Preston Nutter. My brother Clair spent many years during his youth hunting deer on the Nutter ranch and visiting with Nutter's descendants.

Our reunion group had four vehicles, a small camp trailer and five flat tires. As we drove out of the canyon I mentioned to my wife that I could read the Indian Rock Art on the walls above us. I told her it said, "Shoot out the tires of those city dudes who are kicking up so much dust." she just shook her head.

Nine Mile Canyon is north of Wellington but angles toward the canyons of Sunnyside. I had been there once before, deer hunting with Clair and some of the rest of the family. The canyon got it's name from Explorer John Wesley Powell when his crew was surveying in 1879 and used a nine-mile triangulation to measure. Most Utah nine-mile canyons are nine miles from somewhere. Not this one. Although I never traveled from Nine Mile Canyon to the Sunnyside canyons, I know of others who did.

Whitmore Canyon, commonly known as Sunnyside Canyon, was named by George Whitmore who came from Texas in 1878 and began his cattle operation at the mouth of the canyon. He grazed and sold cattle there until 1903, when Pete Jones took over the management of the ranch. The Jones family stayed until 1936. When they moved to Castle Dale, Mr. Swain became the ranch manager. In addition to cattle, the ranching operation also included raising hay, wheat, corn, oats and pigs. The Whitmore ranch covered the area around the Grassy Trail Creek where Dragerton was built in the 1940s.

Number Two Canyon branched out to the southeast at a right angle to Whitmore Canyon in the middle of Sunnyside. The Number Two mine entrance was located here. This canyon was the final location of the barn and corrals operated by the mine company.

Slaughter Canyon was opposite Number Two Canyon. How this short canyon got its name is obvious. The slaughterhouse, first located in Pole Canyon, was re-located here as Sunnyside grew. A few lower town houses were located near the mouth of this canyon.

Hospital Canyon was a small canyon that ran north and east directly behind the Sunnyside School. When fenced in, it was a natural livestock grazing area. In the 1930s and 40s, Uncle Orson Turner used the canyon floor for corrals for his horses and cows. The fenced off area up the hill around Gobblers Knob was where his livestock grazed. This canyon was a popular spot for school field trips, and for hiking and playing when school was not in session.

Up past the asphalt mill and branching off Sunnyside (Whitmore) Canyon to the right is Pasture Canyon. When dad and other horse owners in town were through riding their horses in the fall, they took them to the mouth of Pasture Canyon, turned them loose and the horses wintered in the canyon, thus giving the canyon its name. There was good feed there and most of the winters in this canyon were not too severe. In the spring the horses would begin their migration back to town. Some years when our horse, Old Bolly, made his own way back to the barn, we knew that spring was finally here.

One year in Pasture Canyon, Dick, one of our old horses laid down on his back to dust himself, as horses do. But he apparently picked a spot next to a small ravine, which he then rolled into and couldn't get back out. I discovered his bones the following spring when I went to look for the horses.

A flat, grassy area at the mouth of this canyon was a favorite picnic and ball playing spot for people in Sunnyside. Many town and church picnics were held here. One deer hunting season dad, Clair and brother-in-law Michael hiked up Pasture Canyon and down Number Two Canyon. They saw a few deer but did not shoot any. It was a long, tiring day for them.

North of Pasture Canyon is Pole Canyon. This was a good canyon for gathering Christmas trees. There were a few long-needled Ponderosa Pines in this canyon. The first Sunnyside slaughterhouse had been located at the mouth of this canyon.

The next canyon to the north is Bear Canyon. I've asked a number of people but none of them know how this canyon got its name. It's assumed that bears were spotted in this canyon by early settlers but I'd like to add my own fanciful myth. I like to think an early coal miner was hunting deer in the canyon on his day off. My story continues with him shooting a deer on one side of the canyon from the opposite side. I like to think that before the miner could get across to his deer, a bear happened on the scene and had the deer for his dinner, chasing the miner out of the canyon. Why didn't the miner shoot the bear? He'd used his last bullet on the deer. That may not be history but it makes a good story for telling around a campfire.

Still going north up Whitmore Canyon between the Forks and Bear Canyon is found Box Springs. This was an excellent place to camp as the springs supplied us with fresh water and there was a level area where we could put up our tents or play ball.

North of Box Springs and around the turn, Whitmore Canyon forks. Whitmore Canyon continues to the left and Water Canyon forks to the right. This canyon was more commonly known as Asphalt Canyon because the asphalt quarry sat at the head of it. The three and a half mile tram that transported asphalt to the discharge is still visible. It's quite an engineering marvel when you consider the antiquated equipment with which it was built. If another oil embargo becomes a reality in the future, perhaps the millions of barrels of oil that remain trapped in the rocks in this canyon will create an interest once again.

About five hundred yards from these forks, and up Whitmore Canyon, is where we, and Utah Fuel Company officials, cleared the hillside and established a ski tow operation in the late 1940s. The A frames we used are still visible up on the hillside.

A little over a mile from the discharge forks are the Main Forks. They were called the Right Hand Fork and the Left Hand Fork, for obvious reasons.

The Right Hand Fork is where the majority of water comes that flows down Grassy Trail Creek. This is where much of the early floods began as they wreaked havoc so often to so much of Sunnyside during my youth. In the 1960s, the town and mining company finally obtained the water rights to the creek and built a reservoir at The Forks.

The Forks was a flat, shady, grassy spot that was a favorite place for picnics and camping. As Boy Scouts, we held several camping events at this site. We also camped there, along with many others, on the Friday evenings before the opening day of fishing season. In the Right Hand Fork was where the good fishing holes were located. It was a good grazing area and the canyon was full of quaking aspens. Visitors to the canyon often carved their names or initials in the trees.

Some day I'm going back and find the tree where Martin Rodosh and I carved our names and the names of Ardyth Gibson and Katy Niemeyer. We later married these girls. If I can find that tree and the names are still legible, I may see about harvesting it and placing the carved section in my backyard. Then again, at my age maybe younger generations will have to do this, if it's to get done.

As a boy, I didn't spend much time in the Left Hand Fork Canyon, but I did know that further up that canyon and onto the ridge was the route used by the Pressett boys when they took their loaded pack horses and made the trek to Nine Mile Canyon. And that brings us full circle in remembering Sunnyside's canyons. They hold some great memories for those who ever spent any time in them.

PICNICS

May is one of my favorite months. Some members of the animal kingdom come out of hibernation. So do picnics. In Sunnyside we used to welcome spring by having an annual school celebration, May Day, the first of May. We took part in Maypole dances, races and picnics. From the first grade on, picnics and field trips took place in May.

During May, school teachers planned and supervised the picnics, but after that it was whoever you could get. We even scheduled many of our own picnics without adult supervision. All we needed was a buddy or two, some matches and wood, and a potato each. But more on this later.

The older members of our family were lucky while growing up. They got an unscheduled picnic whenever mother was "going to be sick." When they returned home from the picnic they met their new baby brother or sister. The picnic was at Box Springs when Grant, the youngest child, was born. I got to go, too, although at eighteen months of age there's not much of that picnic I remember.

School picnics in our elementary school days were usually held up the canyon. Sometimes they were held at the mouth of Pasture Canyon. Other times they were held at Box Springs (a little farther up the canyon), or way up the canyon to The Forks. These last two locations required transportation.

Once we hiked up behind the school building to Hospital Canyon. I remember this one because we saw some deer and Mr. Wycherly, our teacher, pointed out the "shell conglomerate" rocks that bubbled when hydrochloric acid was poured on them. On a test later, one class member answered that it was hydraulic acid, and we all had a good laugh.

When we got to junior high, picnics were held at these same spots plus the flat, open area where the Sunnyside Park is now located—the old Whitmore/Pete Jones ranch, and at several locations near the Columbia Dugway.

When I was in eighth grade I put my arm around Norma Harvey's waist as we walked home from one of these picnics. It was a long walk and I'm not sure the picnic fun was worth the walk, but when you're young and in love, no walk is too long.

During the warm summer months we held several impromptu picnics near our woodpile in the backyard or down by the creek in upper town. At these picnics, friends would gather with their potatoes, we'd build a fire, and after sitting around telling war stories until there were enough coals so we could bury our potatoes in them, we'd put the potatoes under the hot coals. After twenty minutes or so we'd eat our hot, dry, dirty potatoes. Most of the times they weren't cooked clear through, but who cared? We were having fun! We'd eat the hot potato as we peeled down the burnt skin, much like eating a banana. With sooty hands and faces and the water canteen empty, the picnic would come to an end. We had several of these 'potato roasts' each summer.

On the Fourth of July after the festivities, our family would drive up the canyon for a picnic, joining with other families for horseshoes, baseball and other activities. Every family brought lots of food and homemade rootbeer and a huge bonfire was built for those lucky enough to have hot dogs and marshmallows to roast.

On Labor Day it was off to Price to the parade and picnic in the park. Good Democrats (and who wasn't?) would sit close to the stage so they could hear the Union leader or politician give his speech. If they mentioned F.D.R. or John L. Lewis it made dad's day. That night, worn out and sleepy, we piled into the car for the ride back to Sunnyside, with dad commenting all the way on what a good talk it had been.

When we turned twelve and got to go to Mutual (the L.D.S. program for adolescents) we got to go to a whole bunch of new picnics. These were always arranged in age groups and then, about the time that we learned there were other interesting females besides our mothers and sisters, we went coed and the really fun times began. Picnics would be held on the church lawn or anywhere else large enough to accommodate a group of young people, like the tennis court, school gym, or the grassy area near the hospital.

We did a lot of gathering in Sunnyside in those early days. I'm not sure how others define picnic, but I'll tell you what it has always meant to me. A picnic is an event where two or more people gather for fun and games. It can be held either when the sun is up or when the sun goes down and there are always food, friends and fun.

All our picnics involved family, relatives or friends. The only thing I ever remember doing alone was going to the outhouse. Maybe I slept alone until I outgrew the crib, but after that it was sleeping between Ned and Clair, and later with Grant in a double bed.

Some of my grandkids have bedrooms that are as large as some of the Sunnyside houses were. Life isn't fair. But then again, maybe it is. Nobody locked doors or cars or anything else when I was young. And the only drive-by shootings taking place were when a deer was sighted from your lookout spot on the mountain during the annual deer hunt.

Before serious courting took place, we teenagers gathered at the drop of a hat. We met most evenings, holidays, birthdays and other summer days when chores were finished.

With a shortage of wheels as we grew older, it was not uncommon to find ten or twelve exuberant teenagers riding in the same car to events. Wheels and gas equaled popularity. From the tenth grade on, when I got my first car, a Model A Ford, I had plenty of friends and no money. And yet, it was funny how there was no one around when you pulled up to the gas station with the needle on empty.

As high school graduation neared and many of us began serious dating, it was still two or three couples traveling in the same car to the picnic or other event. On our picnic and fishing trip to Range Creek, we took three cars, eight guys and our dates. We left town at 1 a.m. My date's dad was a little concerned, but after a short 'prayer meeting' with him, he gave his approval and we were off to Range Creek. We drove in the dark, fished by morning light, ate lunch mid-morning and by noon each of us was by ourselves and sound asleep. The picnic area looked like Custer's Last Stand.

Picnics today just aren't the same. It's off to the park with the family and grandkids, but some can't make it because of Little League, others must leave early because they have to go to dancing practice, still others have a date, and those of us who are older don't like to drive after dark anymore.

During the Sunnyside picnics we stayed as long as possible because when we got home there were always chores to do: cows and horses must be fed; cows needed to be milked and the milk bottled and delivered; wood and coal had to be brought in; and on and on. Too, when some of the picnics ended there was the long drive home.

Picnics and outings are great family activities and I highly recommend them, even today with our fast-paced lifestyles. The trouble is well worth the effort and I believe in that saying that I saw stuck on somebody's fridge, "The families that play together, stay together."

PRANKS, TRICKS
AND PRACTICAL JOKES

We had a cookout in our back yard with some of our long-time friends. We've all lived long enough to have wrinkles, gray hair, and some of us even have a catch in our get-along. As we recalled the funny events in our lives, I was reminded of some of the funny happenings that took place in Sunnyside as I was growing up. Some of life's humorous events are spontaneous, some become funny quite by accident, and still others take a great deal of careful planning to ensure a successful outcome.

One of those planned, successful outcomes was when dad and his nephew, Wade, conceived a plan to fool their co-workers into thinking that the company appreciated their crew and was rewarding them with a box of chocolates.

Dad and Wade worked at the tipple dropping cars. As the coal slack came off the conveyor belts and down the chutes into the large railroad cars, the car droppers would loosen the car brakes just enough for it to roll down the tracks so another slack pile could build up alongside the pile already in the car. When the car was full of slack, it would be let down the tracks and another empty car would be dropped into place and the filling would begin all over again.

There were usually four to six men on each crew and they spent about as much time sitting in the little warming hut as they did dropping cars, so they had time to tell stories and conjure up creative pranks. It was during one of these waiting times that dad and Wade planned their "Company Reward" scheme.

After work, they went to the company store and purchased a one pound box of cherry chocolates. Then around our kitchen table, using a sharp knife, they very carefully cut the bottom of each chocolate and removed the cherry and flavoring inside. With the inside removed, dad and Wade skillfully filled the chocolate shell with cup grease, which was used to grease the railroad car wheels, then pressed the bottom layer of the chocolate back on and put it back in the wrapper and into the box. It took them a couple of hours to re-do the twenty-four cherry chocolates.

The next day at work they placed the box of chocolates on the bench in the hut and told each worker that it was a gift from the company because of the outstanding car dropping their shift had done.

Hungry miners didn't always worry much about social graces. One co-worker had three chocolates between his mouth and stomach before he mentioned that they tasted a little rancid and must be old chocolates. A split second later he knew he had been had and tried to spit the chocolates out, but they were too far gone. By then dad and Wade were falling off the bench with laughter. They then swore that victim to secrecy and the joke was repeated on the entire crew one at a time. The chocolates were all consumed or spit up at the last minute. Everyone laughed around the mine and union hall for weeks over this prank.

About a year later, when memories had faded, dad and Wade were up to their practical jokes again when they did a similar thing with a dozen bottles of Coke. They emptied out the pop and replaced it with used engine oil. The color was about the same but the liquid was slightly thicker.

This time around, dad or Wade would pop the cap off a bottle that had been chilled in a bucket of ice and casually offer it to a crew member. One newcomer had a third of the drink dispatched before he could get it stopped. Once a victim got over the surprise, he wanted to be part of catching the next victim so the joke continued through the shift and involved all the crew that hot summer day.

Dad and Wade were very careful not to accept food or drink gifts from co-workers after that. The two pulled off a few more successful tricks during their time together while working at the tipple. They both loved a good practical joke. And so did the men they worked with.

Wade was killed while dropping cars in 1945 and dad and all of us lost both a good friend and a loved relative.

During my senior year in high school, I tried out for the high school basketball team but didn't make it through the first cut. I still wanted to play so I joined a home team that played in the recreational league. We played our home games in the Dragerton school gym. The spectator chairs were placed around the gym right next to the out of bounds lines.

During one popular game, there was a good crowd on hand and midway through the game the ball went out of bounds. I stepped out and got the ball and was set to throw it in to a team mate. I was standing just in front of where my younger brother Grant was seated with his girl friend.

Just as the ball left my hands, Grant grabbed the bottom sides of my basketball trunks and gave them a yank. Since the waistband was elastic, the trunks dropped down to my knees as my momentum carried me out onto the floor. It was like being hobbled but I stayed on my feet, maintained my composure as I pulled the trunks back to their respectable position and continued on as though nothing had happened. The crowd hooted and hollered as I tried to hide my embarrassment. Some thirty-five years later, an old dude I didn't even know back then reminded me of that event. By then I could laugh about it, too.

When we gathered uptown for night games we often met

on Uncle Orson's south lawn. The cement retaining wall surrounding their lawn was about three feet high and made for a nice place to sit and visit. Roy Davis lived in the second house from the school on back street. He always joined us for the games. He had a large old spotted dog named Duke which was almost big enough to pass for a pinto horse. He was about that color.

Aunt Bernice had a nice flower garden next to her house and when old Duke had the urge he always went to that flower bed, raised his leg, and did his thing.

One evening, he did his thing just as Aunt Bernice appeared on the back porch. She got her broom and went after Duke, but Duke knew when to run and when to poke along. As Aunt Bernice went back toward the screen door she called to her son who was working on a nearby car, "Phillip, can't you do something about that dog always peeing on my flowers?"

Phillip said he could and would. He turned to Roy and said, "Bring that dog by tomorrow at six, after I get off work."

Later that same evening, Phillip got some thin thread-like copper wire and stretched it among the flowers. He attached one end to a Model A Ford coil and attached the coil to a battery. He carefully concealed everything.

At six the next evening we all showed up. Phillip gave us a wink and told us to act normal but watch the flower bed. Sure enough, it wasn't long until old Duke cocked his leg in preparation for his ritual. When the pee hit the wire, ZAP!, Duke's hind legs went straight in the air and he let out a yelp louder than we knew a dog could yelp. He was still squawking thirty minutes later as he sat near his dog house in Roy's back yard.

Aunt Bernice came out to see what all the commotion

was about. Phillip asked her if she had any more problems needing fixing. Old Duke never went near the flowers again. In fact, old Duke did not join Roy for night games at all after that.

A year or so later, when Grant got his "new" 1937 Chev coupe and a couple of his friends started scuffling in the front seat, he got an idea. During the next ride when the scuffling began, he asked them to stop. They didn't, so Grant hit a button under the dashboard and ZAP!, his two friends hit the ceiling of that coupe and scuffling in Grant's car ended forever. Grant had borrowed that coil from Phillip and it did the job.

I've heard about and seen some of the tricks my kids and their kids have played and I realize that practical jokes and pranks don't change much over the years. Telling about them does. They get better with every telling.

RANGE CREEK

To a youngster, some places appear to be far away and have a bit of mystery surrounding them. Sort of a never-never land where only the lucky or wealthy ever get to visit. Like Disneyland, the ocean, the North Pole, the Old Country, Hawaii or places like that. Range Creek was in that category when I was growing up.

Range Creek was far away. There was a certain romance to the name. My dad promised to take me there when I "got bigger." My older brothers had been there or were going there in the near future. Later, I learned that it wasn't such a special place after all, but I didn't know that at the time.

Range Creek was the stream across the mountain about ten miles from town that supplied the drinking water for Sunnyside. The water had to be pumped over the mountain. The only way to get to Range Creek was by trail up Number Two Canyon and then over the mountain.

Although I ended up visiting the place twice, apparently I was not very observant or impressed on either trip since I don't remember many details about the place, itself. There was the operator's small residence, an ordinary sort of dwelling, and the pump house. The pump house contained a large motor and pump that forced the water through the pipe up and over the mountain.

About one and a half miles up Number Two Canyon was a large concrete water collection tank. From the tank, gravity was the force that brought the water down into town. As younsters, many of us made several trips to the water tank. But no further.

Part of the Range Creek mystique evolved around the Olsen family. They had the contract to take supplies from the company store in Sunnyside to Range Creek twice a month when the trail was not snowed in. The supplies were taken by pack horses and mules.

As I recall, Henning Olsen was the father and John and Lloyd were his sons. They did most of the trail riding as near as I can remember. They all wore chaps, spurs and cowboy boots and hats. They were almost larger than life in the eyes of an eight year old boy.

When the loading took place, the pack animals were tied to a telephone pole above the railroad tracks just northwest of the store. Sheepherder "Shorty Nick" and "cowpoke" Danny Collins tied up at the same spot, as did other horsemen when visiting the company store. I hung around the area often and sometimes the horse's owner would let me hold the reins while he shopped. Whenever I was there, John Olsen would let me hold the reins of his horse. Who needed Roy Rogers' autograph? I held the reins of the horse that would lead the pack train to Range Creek!

Several men would help carry the boxes of supplies from the store to the packing area. There they would load the canvas bags, one on each side of the pack animal and hooked to the pack saddle. Later, in college, I learned that the official name of this canvas bag was a 'pannier.'

Other items such as clothing, gloves, ropes, wire, tools and an assortment of odds and ends would accompany the food in the panniers. The Olsens would load first thing in the morning, as soon as the store opened, and then start up Number Two Canyon, arriving at Range Creek in the early evening. They would return a day or two later. This process was repeated over and over again through the years. I looked forward to hanging around the area each time they were getting ready for the Range Creek trip.

Ned Arambula, a former boxer and a leader of young

men and boys, arrived in town in the early 1940s during World War II. I didn't know it at the time but he would be the one to lead my first trip to Range Creek.

Ned assumed the duties of keeping all the interested young boys in Sunnyside and Sunnydale physically and mentally fit. He had us boxing, tumbling, exercising and running during most of our free time. He also had us hiking often. One autumn, when I was approaching my teen years, he surprised us by announcing that the first trip the next summer would be an overnighter to Range Creek. Here was our chance to see that fabled place. We anxiously waited for the slow winter to pass that year.

There were only two events that happened on our hike to Range Creek that summer that were permanently etched on my mind. I'm sure that many things happened that were noteworthy, but time has erased most of them. The things that did make an impression were the two-quart bottle of peaches and the rain storm.

As my younger brother, Grant, and I packed our homemade packs for the trip, I made a trip to our fruit cellar for a two-quart bottle of peaches which we would share during one of our meals while on the hike.

Hiking up Number Two Canyon to the water tank was reasonably gradual, but once we started up the mountain, that was another story. It was steep, rocky and hard climbing. I believe that my pack took on additional weight as we climbed—at least that's the way it felt. Halfway up the mountain on one of our rest stops, I fiddled with my pack, pretending to adjust it. What I was really doing was fishing for that ten pound bottle of peaches. When no one was looking, I slid the bottle of peaches under a bush thinking that I would reclaim it on the return trip.

We had eaten breakfast at 6 a.m. with the lunch break scheduled for when we reached the top of the mountain.

We reached the top about 2 p.m., found a shady spot, and began digging out our lunches from our packs.

Grant said, "Why don't we eat some of the peaches now? It will help lighten your load." I replied, "Let's save them for later." With that we dug out, and prepared to eat, our smashed sandwiches.

As we began eating, Ned, who held the rear position on the trail, appeared at the hill top. We all invited him to come and sit by us while he ate his lunch. He headed in my direction and, as he passed by, stopped long enough to slip me a half concealed bottle of peaches. With a wink he quietly said, "This must have dropped out of your pack. I'm sure that you and Grant can use it."

I called out to Grant, who was sitting a few feet away, indicating that I had dug the peaches out of my pack and that we could eat them now. After consuming two quarts of peaches, we two brothers were stuffed. Ned Arambula was one of my heroes before the trip but he became an even bigger one on that day.

The other event that will always be remembered by me was that before lunch was finished we got a downpour that made Noah's flood look like the morning dew. It came down in sheets. This one lasted only forty minutes, not forty days. We finally finished drying out around the campfire that evening at Range Creek.

We hiked back to town the next day. My curiosity had been satisfied. I had been to Range Creek.

A few years later the mine company opened the Horse Canyon Mine south of Sunnyside and completed a road on to Range Creek. For all practical purposes, having to hike to Range Creek was now a thing of the past. With this new road into Range Creek, another of the mysterious wonders of the world passed into history.

As my days in Sunnyside were coming to an end, several of us young men and our dates took an early morning ride on this new road to Range Creek for a day of fishing, picnicking, and partying. We completed the fishing and picnicking part with no trouble but the partying part was spent sprawled out under whatever shade we could find catching up on the sleep we had missed by leaving so early in the morning. This, too, was an eventful Range Creek trip because later on I married my Range Creek date.

Perhaps if the back-to-nature enthusiasts have their way, Range Creek will be designated as wilderness and we'll go back to the good old days. Heaven forbid this should happen; I'll have to hike back up the old trail and retrieve that empty two-quart bottle.

But then again, with modern trail foods, lightweight camping gear and accurate weather forecasting, that trip might not be half bad. My past could become my future if that happens.

RECYCLING

I was in the big city the other day and spotted an acquaintance putting his garbage out by the curb. He had placed several different colored bins by his garbage container and as I got closer I could see that each bin had the type of contents written on the side. One was for aluminum, one was for newspapers, another said plastic and the final label read glass. He had also bundled some limbs that were cut to three feet lengths.

This man was discarding in the trash more items than we had in our whole house in Sunnyside when I was a boy. If our waste was absolutely no longer usable it went over the creek bank or, in the case of stove ashes, out into the dusty, weed-strewn alley behind the house. We used and re-used most items then used what was left for fuel in our wood/coal burning stoves. If we were to eat, the kitchen stove had to be fired up even during the hot summer days.

The only tree trimming was done by the wind. If it blew hard enough to take branches out of a tree, we would cut the limbs into stove size logs, use the smaller branches for kindling and throw the leaves over the creek bank. Mulch? Without a garden, no need.

Any metal went into the scrap iron pile which was hauled to the junkyard in Price and turned into cash at $3 a ton. Insulated wire had the insulation burned off and went into the copper stack where it fetched two cents a pound. The few metal cans we ever had to discard were put to other uses. An empty tuna can made a great candle holder when the power went out, which was fairly often in that windy canyon town. Empty canned milk cans were hammered onto the bottom of our shoes for us to stomp around on during make-believe games. I know it sounds dumb, but we kids took our fun any way we could get it. Larger empty cans held nails and other stuff on the cellar, barn and garage shelves.

Paper sacks from the store were re-used for school lunches, to store old rags (the key word here is OLD; we wore the stillgood rags), and to hide the hard-tack Christmas candy until what was left of it (we kids always found it soon after it was hidden) was put in our stockings Christmas Eve. Paper sacks were smaller in those days. No one could afford the large bags of groceries like we carry out of the supermarket today. When the sack was torn or liquid had seeped out the bottom, weakening it, it was used to start the fire in the stove. Plastic bags were not to show up for another generation or two.

Out of date catalogs were always saved and stacked in our outhouse for use as toilet paper. This was neater than it sounds because we always had reading material at hand while we were there.

Newspapers were saved for re-use in a number of ways. They made good crumbled-up towels when washing windows. The ink actually made the window panes shine brighter. Windex was unheard of in those days. Warm water, clean rags and newspapers were all we ever needed. Even today, articles on window washing often include the value of vinegar water and newspaper for shiny, unstreaked windows. When we finished washing the windows the damp newspaper was dried and saved to start fires in the stoves.

Newspapers, too, were always spread out on the kitchen table when mother cleaned the chickens for Sunday dinner. Chicken insides, feathers and everything else to be discarded was wrapped in the soggy newspapers and popped into the stove. The additional smoke and smell was the trade off for the heat generated.

We didn't have wastebaskets in my early days. There was no waste to put in any. No disposals, either. Fruit came in bottles. All empty bottles were washed and used again and again until they broke. Every bit of food on the table was eaten. If there was anything left over from a meal it was eaten the next meal. No pick and choose at our table. It was like windmill soup—if it came around, you got some. We learned to like almost everything except hunger. We had enough food but few choices.

Mother used to make what we all called "cherry bean soup." Nobody knows the origin of that name, we just remember really enjoying that soup. A few years before she died, we told mother how we remembered and relished that soup with a slice of her delicious, homemade, whole wheat bread. She laughed as she told us how it came to be. Because we had cows, we nearly always had milk. Some of her sisters lived on farms in other small towns and they often sent us boxes of fresh vegetables from their gardens when they were harvested so onions were usually plentiful. But sometimes there was not much else but beans, good old kidney beans. So when we were low on supplies, mother cooked the beans until they were tender, mashed them, added diced onions, salt and pepper, and slowly stirred in milk until the soup thickened and turned deep pink in color. That was "cherry bean soup." Her creation not only satisfied our hunger but actually gave us pleasure. Mother was a creative cook. She had to be.

Today we scrape more food off the plates and into the garbage after a big Sunday dinner than we ever had for dinner in the early days. Of course we do that with all our materials possessions these days.

We recycled toys long ago, too. If a pair of roller skates got broken we took the remaining wheels and made a wooden scooter. When the scooter wore out the metal went into the scrap iron pile, the 2x4s returned to the wood pile and the nails were straightened and saved for the next project. Discarded baby buggy wheels and empty orange crates made great go-carts, and stilts were easy to make with a couple of 2x4s, some blocks of wood and a few straightened nails.

Our home in Provo was built in the 1930s from two empty Sunnyside houses which were sold to interested buyers who were willing to dismantle and remove them. Everything possible from these houses, including the nails, was saved for re-use in Provo. Everyone in the family was involved. I remember that even us little kids could hammer bent nails fairly straight and chop wood scraps into kindling for the stove. The backyard of the Provo home still contains several big square rocks that are now used as seats, but were once footings for mine car trestles at the original tipple in Sunnyside. Dad reclaimed them in his later years and hauled them to Provo.

In those early days, if the item in your hand had no recycle value, it was taken to the creek bank and thrown over the side. The creek was the ultimate recycler. The items thrown over the bank would get a gravity boost, working their way to the creek bed. The July and August thunderstorms caused flooding each year taking creek bed, banks and everything else in the way and depositing them under tons of silt somewhere below town, thus returning them to Mother Earth. A million years from now archeologists may dig down several feet through the topsoil and learn about the culture of our ancient town. It's a thought.

As I finished the curbside visit with my friend, I got to thinking that we recycled years ago, only in a different way. Our discard bins were the scrap iron pile, woodpile, bent-nail and reclaimed screws storage cans, newspaper stack on the back porch, the stove, or over the creek bank. No landfills or curbside picking up for our unusable junk. We had a place for everything.

The newspaper the next day said that the nuclear waste people in Washington were still looking for a dump site. If the EPA would leave us alone I believe we could use the old Sunnyside creek. Then again, maybe not.

SCOUTING

Last week in church they announced that the scouts were getting ready for summer camp. I said a silent prayer of thanks that I was not the scoutmaster, and that I would not have to go with the scouts to camp for a week. I've had my turn and it was great. But at my age the noise, half-cooked food and hard ground to sleep on would certainly, I feel, hasten an attack of some kind. And that would definitely ruin the trip for everyone. However, when I was a boy . . .

During World War II, I became old enough to join the Boy Scouts. There was one problem, though. We had no scout troop in Sunnyside and all the potential scoutmasters were serving their country.

My older brothers had mentioned that Mac McKinley had been their scout leader years ago. I knew that Mac worked in the office at the asphalt mill. Although he had reached the age where he shouldn't have had to worry about leading a bunch of adolescent boys, I visited with him anyway. "You are the only one in town who can be our scoutmaster. Will you do it?"

He said yes, but then asked if I had the authority to issue the call.

I replied, "We don't need authority, just your okay." I then told our bishop what I'd done and he made the call official.

In those days, the Boy Scouts of America was closely connected with the L.D.S. Church as it was the only institution specifically organizing scout troops and scouting activities in the area. Membership in the church wasn't required for boys to join church-sponsored troops and ours was a broadly heterogeneous group.

Mac led us for the next two years. We met every Tuesday at Mutual in the church for scout meeting. By the time we were officially organized I was the oldest boy in the troop so there was no objection when I was appointed Senior Patrol Leader.

One of the requirements for First Class rank was to do the Scout Pace in ten minutes. This was described in the handbook as the method used in an emergency to go for help. You ran one hundred steps and walked one hundred steps, then ran one hundred steps again, etc. until you completed the required distance. You had to do this in ten minutes. You could not miss it by more than thirty seconds either way. It took me three times to learn to do it in ten minutes, but from then on I was the troop expert on the Scout Pace.

To get the distance correct I had dad drive me in the truck while we watched the speedometer. First we left the church and went down to the tennis court, made a right turn, and another right turn at main street. Up past the school for another right, and the final right on back street to the church. Not quite a mile, so we swung down by the store and back to the church to get it exactly one mile. After I passed it off, I ran and walked with each scout in the troop until he hit it right near the ten minute mark. The whole troop became experts at the Scout Pace.

Another requirement for First Class was learning the Morse Code. It was two years later, when camping with the Explorers in our Provo Manavu Ward, that I finally saw this code put to good use. Harold Bailey, the long-time Manavu Explorer Leader, took the scouts hiking and fishing in the High Uinta Mountains each summer. One summer, while we were staying in Provo, I was invited along.

After hiking about ten miles we arrived at (I believe) Pinto Lake. I noticed that Leader Bailey sent two older scouts, named Richardson and Pendleton, on hiking up another mountain as the rest of us stopped for camp and fishing. I inquired as to where they were going. Leader Bailey said, "You'll see tonight at 9 p.m."

Sure enough, at 9 p.m. he had us gather around the campfire and said, "Go get your pencils and paper ready and watch the ridge to the south."

Shortly a flashlight was seen blinking on the mountain top just as it was getting dark. Leader Bailey said, "They are going to send a message. Tell me what it says."

I remembered the Morse Code and as the flashing began I wrote down, F-I-S-H-I-N-G G-O-O-D C-O-M-E O-N U-P. The signaling stopped and Bailey said, "Right after breakfast we'll break camp and hike to Pine Island Lake."

The scouts had signaled that the fishing was good, and it was. We brought home a gunnysack full of fish. That was a great Explorer group.

Back in Sunnyside, Mac McKinley took me with him to all of the training sessions conducted by the District and Council scout leaders. I got acquainted with Commissioner Madsen from Price, professional scouters Anderson and Doman, and national trainer Bob Perrin, who I met again on many occasions when I joined professional scouting many years later.

Our Sunnyside troop did a lot of camping. In those days we weren't much on advancement once a member became a First Class Scout. I did earn my five merit badges and became a Star Scout before advancing to Sports, Exploring and, later, girls. This part of the program hasn't changed much over the years.

When Mac moved away, a Mr. Croft became our scoutmaster for a very short time. Then, a few months later, it was Andy Anderson. Dad and William Walker, the new mine superintendent, were on the troop committee and attended some of our scout meetings when we held them in the Sunnydale City Offices building.

One year dad took a load of us scouts in the back of his stake truck on a scouting trip to Ferron Reservoir. Several other troops were there and we had a great time together.

The Carbon Stake Young Men conducted a trip to Yellowstone National Park one summer. We rode on seats put in the back of a large cattle truck. There were more than forty boy scouts riding in the back of that truck. Our camping and personal gear were in another large dump truck. Several leaders accompanied us in cars. We camped along the way for two nights, finally arriving at the West Thumb campground at Yellowstone.

Several events about that trip come to mind. One was when two older guys riding in the seats at the front of the truck threw a cube of butter at a car coming in the opposite direction. The cube hit the car windshield and the driver made a speedy u-turn and stopped our truck. After our leaders learned what had happened we had a real "prayer meeting" and were told we'd go right home if that, or anything like it, happened again. The trip was pretty routine after that.

At West Thumb, Grant and I put on our swimming trunks and waded out into Yellowstone Lake to fish. I hooked a fish on my line and a passing driver stopped by the side of the road to watch the action. I didn't have a fishing net so I was working my way out of the water, trying to keep the fish on the line. We had waded in up to our armpits.

When I was out of the water to my waist, the man watching yelled, "Don't come any further—my wife is watching.""

I called back, "Let her watch," and continued on out of the lake. He gave a sigh of relief when he saw that I had on swimming trunks. He thought I'd been fishing in the nude.

On that same trip, Grant and his group tried to catch a

bear but things didn't work out, so they gave up. Lucky for them. That was another great scout trip.

In the mid-1940s the Scout Council in Provo announced that they had just purchased Camp Maple Dell in Payson Canyon. They invited troops to go camping there. Dad took several of us from our Provo Ward to the camp that summer, the first scouts to camp at that new scout camp. One end of the lake was full of frogs, so Grant and a friend caught several and feasted on fried frogs legs for a couple of meals. That particular delicacy didn't appeal to me at all so I dined out of the cans and bottles we had brought from home.

Scouting and the outdoors has always held a special place in my heart. I guess that is why it was easy for me to make the change from Elementary Education to Scouting and Youth Leadership when B.Y.U. introduced this new program in 1956 while I was attending college. In 1957 I joined the Utah National Parks Council as a new District Scout Executive. I served in this capacity for sixteen years, enjoying every minute of it. Our own seven sons all became Eagle Scouts.

When Mac McKinley accepted the job as Sunnyside Scoutmaster again, he opened the way for so many outdoor experiences I may have missed had he refused. I was fortunate to be around good scout leaders as I grew up, from Mac and my dad through Ned Arambula, another great scoutmaster. I've met even more as a camp director and professional scouter.

The policies have changed. Scouts don't ride in the back of trucks anymore, and mothers don't have to make backpacks like our mother had to do for Grant and me. Even the food has changed. Scouts don't carry bottles of peaches from home like we did. One thing that hasn't changed, though, is the goal of character building that has always been the major plan of scouting. "On my honor..." May it ever be so.

SKIING

It was late August and the TV Weather Reporter said, "You skiers get ready. There was a dusting of snow on Park City's mountains as a storm moved through the area." I knew we'd soon see the ads for the pre-season sales on ski equipment and clothes, and we'd be into another ski season. This is one of the great things about living in an area with four seasons. With the Winter Olympic Games coming to Utah in the year 2002, we'll get another opportunity to see just how far skiing and winter sports have come during the past fifty plus years.

In Sunnyside my older brothers used barrel staves as their first skis, nailing leather strips on them to slide their shoes into. They tried to ski down the boulder-strewn mountain behind our house but Clair says they walked more than glided on those staves. Then Dean found two discarded six feet long floor boards, cut and sawed one end of each board into points, steamed those ends until they were pliable and braced them in a doorjamb until they dried into upturned points. Then he nailed a wide leather strip across the middle of each, just big enough for shoes to fit in and, voila!, a real pair of skis!

Besides skiing on them himself, Dean taught Ned and Clair to use them. At this point let's pick up an entry from mother's diary. "December 28, 1936 (blizzard today, clear tonight) A bad accident happened today. Ned, Dean and Clair were out skiing on the mountain behind our house. Ned, hit a rock, flew into the air and down landing on his back on the rock. A ski broke. Dean carried Ned into the house. He was very pale and couldn't move. He walks some now tonight." No bones were broken and Ned was soon over his fall.

Someone must have made a new ski to replace the broken one because we had a pair of old wooden skis around the garage for as long as I can remember. They reminded me of elf shoes with the pointed toes. There were no bindings, just leather straps that went across the top of your overshoes. We used these old skis in the winter for a straight ride from the garage, which was really a cave tunneled out of the mountain, down to the sidewalk. Speed was not a factor for us.

One Christmas Grant and I got a pair of miniature skis. They were about a foot long. Several other kids in town got these as well. Santa must have had a special going on. There was a bit of a hill south of the tennis court. We spent one day there, and the rest of those holidays trying to get someone to pull us on a rope behind their car. By the time school resumed, most of the skis were broken, but our interest in skiing continued to grow.

Serious skiing in our family and town happened at the end of World War II, during the mid-1940s. It was at this time that war surplus items began showing up in the Army and Navy stores in Salt Lake.

We were living in Provo at this time, during one of our two year stints, and we learned of a place in Provo Canyon that had a ski tow rope. The place was called Stewart's Flats, up near Aspen Grove Campground.

Clair, just out of the army, took Grant and me with him to Salt Lake to buy surplus ski equipment and get in on the real fun. Clair and I each bought a pair of skis with the bindings already on. Grant would use the old homemade skis, but bought a pair of metal bindings. We spent the next few days in anticipation of Saturday when Clair would drive us up to the ski area. We mounted the bindings on Grant's skis. Those old leather straps now became history. We even waxed our skis with the wax we had bought because the salesman told us we'd need it.

Ski clothes were a far cry from today's color-coordinated ski fashions. We bought war surplus ski boots. The smallest available were size 12. We overcame this with five pairs of wool socks. We used our regular old denim pants, sweatshirts and jackets and deer hunting caps, and we were off to the slopes.

On our first trip up the hill we watched all of the skiers on the slopes making turns and going slowly down the hill. We let go of the tow rope and headed down the hill in a straight line, which was a change for us with no boulders to veer around. Our problem was where and how to stop at the bottom. We did a lot of falling and sliding that first day before we learned the Snowplows and related movements to get down the hill.

With each trip we gained a little more skill and knowledge. Stewarts added a second tow. It was a cable tow. We were furnished with a metal hook, tied to a short rope which was in turn tied to the center of a small round wooden seat, almost resembling a broom handle. The idea was to let the cable slide through the hook until you were ready to go. When you were ready you straddled the wooden bar seat, leaned back on it and the cable pulled you up the hill. Getting your hook and rope off the cable took precision and a good jerk at the right time. When not on the tow, you tied the rope with hook and seat around your waist. If you fell wrong you could count on a couple of sharp, jabbing pains. OSHA would never approve this equipment today.

The kind of skiing we did took its toll. One of Grant's skis broke off right behind the binding. We cut the other ski off at the same place so they matched, and he looked like he had on long elf shoes. Being the fun-loving, good sport he was, he made the best of this. While others were waiting in line for their turn at the tow, Grant could run across the top of everyone's skis and hook right up to the tow. Everyone, including Grant, had a good laugh.

When we moved back to Sunnyside in 1948, skiing was taking hold there, too, and we encouraged it. We needed a smooth hillside and tow in Sunnyside so several of us got together and formed the Bruin Mountain Ski Club. Some of the original officers were John McFarland, Martin Rodosh, Johnny Preston, Kendall Nelson, Grant and me. We approached Mine Superintendent, Bob Heers, with our request. We had located a side hill just beyond the Forks at the discharge. Bob sent a D-8 Cat and crew to the site to help clear it and we were in business.

I believe our first tow included an old Model A Ford with an extra rim on the outside back wheel, with the back wheels in the air. The rope went around the spare rim a couple of times and was anchored on top with another rim hooked to a solid pole. The tow rope was about one or two inches in diameter. We would grab the rope at the bottom of the hill and let go at the top.

Eventually, the company furnished a regular motor that was permanently in place. Over the years the company installed permanent A frames for cable pulley wheels. These are still in place today, although it's been years since anyone has skied on that hill.

I remember one incident well. The tow rope would twist as it pulled you up the hill. We learned to let the twisting rope slide in our hands and not wind up our clothing. Before we became skilled at this, Grant was being pulled up the hill and did not notice as the rope wound up his bulky clothing by his belt. I was at the bottom watching and wondered why he hadn't let go at the right spot. Then he left the ground. With his arms and legs free of the rope, he was dangling in mid-air and headed for the top pulley. I lunged for the shutoff switch and Grant made it safely to the ground. The next day, Bob Heers and his electricians placed a safety device at the top that would turn off the motor automatically in case this happened again.

By this time, at Carbon High School and Carbon College, skiing was catching on with a great deal of student interest. One winter we rented several railroad cars and took the "ski train" to Schofield for a skiing weekend. We also took the college ski team to Snow College for a Meet at a Sanpete County ski slope. I was never much for competition because I didn't feel I was skilled enough yet, but non-competition skiing during my early years was always a great sport.

On one occasion, Dr. Orson Spencer invited a couple of us to go with his family for a weekend to Aspen, Colorado and watch the international F.I.S. ski teams practice. This was a great skiing adventure.

The Provo Canyon area changed from Stewart's Flats to Timp Haven and, finally, to Sundance. The old rope tows have been replaced by electronic ski lifts. Ski clothes are colorful and tight fitting, and today's bindings release when you fall. In the early days, when you fell your skis stayed with you while you were sliding and tumbling down the mountain. Luckily, very few of us in those days ended up with broken bones.

The mine companies in Carbon County were very supportive of the young people in the towns they owned in the early days, and skiing in Sunnyside was just one example of that cooperation.

Skiing has come a long way since those early days of barrel staves, homemade wooden skis and nailed on leather straps. In fact, skiing is one of the few things I know of that gets better with age.

THE STORE

Tennessee Ernie Ford could have recorded his famous song, "Sixteen Tons," from the big porch of the Sunnyside Store because it was one of the company stores that 'owned a coal miner's soul.' We learned early in life about not buying on credit from mother and dad who never did charge anything at the store. They said they saw too many cases of people never getting out of debt there.

Miners could draw scrip from the mine office to be used in place of cash at the store only, or "Charge it!" Cash, itself, was a rare commodity. Competitive pricing was unknown. If you wanted or needed something, you got it at the store.

The store was one of my favorite places while growing up. The store had candy and pop. If we worked dad just right when he took us to the store with him, we got one of each.

The store was in the center of town and from its broad front porch you could see forever. With the town in a canyon, forever goes in just two directions. The mountains blocked the view in the other directions. It was mostly men and boys who gathered on the store porch to shoot the breeze. Only a few 'coarse' women ever joined them there. The rest of the females in town did their visiting inside the store while they shopped.

Ellis Peacock, who worked in the butcher shop (no meat was ever pre-cut and wrapped in those days), was one of my favorite store employees. Once he put a box of moldy candy in the garbage container behind the store. Martin Rodosh and I discovered the box. We scraped the mold from the twenty-four chocolate and caramel bars. For the next few days mother wondered if I was feeling well since my appetite wasn't up to its usual voracity.

Royal Crown Cola was my favorite drink sold at the store until mother said that good Mormons don't drink pop that contains caffeine. I was heart-broken, but I gave up Royal Crown.

At the age of ten I was in love with the beautiful Fabrezio girl who worked as a cashier at the store. Other pretty girls worked there, too. Yvonne Della Corte and Mary Eaquinto, who were Ella Ruth's age, began working at the store when they graduated from high school and they never stopped.

On the store porch, Mike Fratto added to our joy by lighting entire packages of fire crackers and tossing them into the air. He did this many times for a full week before the 4th of Julys of my youth. From the porch we watched the Olsen men load their pack train horses with supplies for the trip to Range Creek. We also watched the trains as their steam engines spun their wheels and belched clouds of steam and black smoke while switching railroad cars from one track to another just west of the store. Sometimes we children would run over and put pennies on those tracks for the train to run over and smash completely flat.

Fresh fruits and vegetables were available at the store only during the growing season—late summer and fall. But sometimes fresh produce was trucked in from outside Utah. Since some of our family meals and most of our midnight snacks consisted of bread and milk, an added banana from the store was a rare treat.

The store was conveniently located near the tipple, the mine entrance and the mine office. Consequently, all the men in town passed the store on their way to and from work. There were no city planners in coal mining towns, but someone understood economics. If there was any money left in your paycheck after the amount you owed the store was taken out, you could pick it up at the mine office fifty yards from the store, cash it there, and walk directly to the store to spend what was left.

In front of the store the road went uphill then curved as it passed the amusement hall. In the winter it was fun to stand on the store porch and watch cars spin and slide on the snow packed road. It was a toss-up where I learned more as a youngster—at my mother's knee or on the porch of the store. No, my mother would win this one.

During World War II a bunkhouse was built southwest of the store for the single men who came to Sunnyside to work in the mines. The bunkhouse was a great place to gather empty, returnable beer bottles and cash them in for neat stuff at the store.

Dante Pederiva was the store manager. He lived just up the street from our house. I always liked to deliver milk or run errands to his house. They kept a bag of hardtack candy handy and always gave us two or three pieces.

In 1944, the old Sunnyside Store closed as a new one opened in Sunnydale, just south of town. Ownership of the store changed from the mining company to Price Trading Company. The new store was called Miner's Trading Post.

One of my good friends, Jim Murphy, worked at the new store. After discarding old produce every day for a few weeks, he suggested that we get some pigs since we now had the food for them. We bought two pigs at the auction in Price and raised them in a pen behind our house. I don't remember if we made any money or not when we sold them at the auction a year later. But I do know we were wiser.

Jim and I switched jobs and I worked at the store for a few months, but the story of that switch is a whole different chapter.

As I visit the malls, the WalMarts and the supermarkets,

I'm amazed and impressed at the number and variety of items that are available. But I still remember fondly the days when, as customers in the old Sunnyside Store, we were called by our first names by every employee in the store.

The company store (right) under construction and the bunk house. (Photo courtesy GEA-USHS)

The railroad depot was built next. (Photo courtesy GEA-USHS)

Later the bunk house was torn down and the mine office and amusement hall took its place. A butcher shop was also built north of the store.
(Photo courtesy USHS)

STRANGE ?

When we were children, little brother Grant and I would get "leg aches." This was an ache and soreness all the way through one of our legs between the ankle and the knee. When this happened, mother would soak a cloth in cold water and salt and wrap that cloth around our leg. She would then wrap a towel around the salt-soaked cloth and pin, with safety pins, it tightly on both ends of the towel. We would then be tucked into bed. The next morning the pain would be gone. We would take the dried towel and cloth off, wipe the dry salt from our leg and be back in full activity. This happened two or three times each month, especially during cold weather. I've never known my kids or grandkids to experience this malady—or the treatment. Only in Sunnyside. Strange??

In perusing the old Town Board Minutes recently I noticed that right after the beginning of World War II, dad got approved the purchase of two Deputy Marshall badges. On two different occasions during this same period of time, I observed that after his day shift at the tipple, and after the chores were done, about dark dad put a small silver pistol into his back overall pocket and walked across the foot bridge toward the tipple and mine. About bedtime he returned.

The pistol was not the Old West type with a long barrel and rotating cylinder for bullets but, instead, a style law enforcement officers carry with a clip in the handle.

As dad was slipping it into his pocket on one occasion, I asked to see it. He showed it to me then put it back into his pocket. I asked what he used it for and where he was going.

He indicated that he was doing a little night shift work around the mine and tipple. I didn't think any more about it at the time but, since then, I've wondered if, as the war was getting more serious, officials might have been concerned about sabotage or other subversive activities, and dad was assigned to watch, just in case. Strange?

During a coal strike in Sunnyside in 1922, the company hired guards to protect the mining property and the men who remained on the job. A gate was erected five miles below town and the light in the lighthouse on the mountain across from the tipple was re-activated. The gate and light were manned by company guards. It was sometime during this period that the company purchased several long-barrel, octagon, 30-30 caliber rifles for use by the guards and those loyal to the company.

During the late 1940s when the company store had been moved to Sunnydale, twenty of these old guns were declared surplus and sold. As a store employee at the time, I got wind of the impending sale and was allowed to purchase one of the guns for $20, the going price.

I used this gun during two deer hunts. The first was when we were hunting at Coal Springs between the asphalt quarry and Range Creek. I was on the side of one mountain looking across the canyon to the other sagebrush covered hillside. A buck moved up from the trees in the bottom to where there was only sagebrush. I began firing the rifle as the buck ran back and forth, confused by the shooting. As it moved up the hillside, I kept shooting and could see dust fly once in awhile. Finally, after about fifteen shots, the deer was hit. I had shot it through the neck for a clean kill. Uncle Orson and his truck and horse showed up and we got that fine, big buck back to camp.

The other occasion with this old gun was after I was married and living in Richfield. Dad came down to hunt with us one season and, along with Klar and Barbara Oldroyd, the four of us left before daylight for Burnt Hollow on Cove Mountain, east of Richfield. It was one of the Oldroyd's favorite hunting spots. We got to Burnt Hollow and started up the hillside. At a sagebrush flat, they pointed out a large boulder at one end of the clearing and indicated that that was where I was to sit until after daylight. Then the three of them disappeared into the thick timber.

Just as it was getting light, four nice bucks appeared at the opposite end of the clearing. What a sight. I waited until they got to the middle of the clearing before I started shooting. They were in line and I decided to shoot the last one first so as not to arouse them. Four shots later I began to have second thoughts. No hits, but the deer were now confused and just walking in circles. This is what every hunter creams about. Now I would wait until two of them were side by side then I'd drop two with one shot. Eight shots later all four bucks were still walking in circles.

Time to reload and go for the front buck. The sagebrush was about waist high and thick so I could not see where the bullets were hitting. One box of bullets (that's twenty four total) later, one buck finally dropped. I kept shooting until the other three wandered out of sight.

Dad, Klar and Barbara, hearing all the shooting, returned just in time to help me find the buck I had hit. Another clean shot through the neck. That was the only deer we got that day. I wondered if that old gun, with non-adjustable sights, was jinxed somehow. I got back to town and talked with "Buck's Sporting Goods" store manager, Jay Thompson. Jay is a nephew of George (Buck) Young, formerly of Sunnyside and Price. After I told my sad story, Jay traded me a new 30-

30 Carbine for that old "Long Tom." I never missed like that again. The story gets better with each telling, but it did really happen. Strange?

When we moved to Provo for two years the first time, dad sent along one of the cows so we would have milk. The cow gave birth to a calf and after the calf was weaned, dad loaded it into his stake truck for the return trip to Sunnyside. At a stop light in Springville, the calf jumped over the four feet high sideboards of the truck and landed on its head on the asphalt street. It lay there, unmoving. Dad assumed it was dead. Another motorist who had stopped when the calf went over the side, helped dad load the lifeless calf back into the truck. Dad said he would drop it in a garbage pit when he got back to Sunnyside. When he arrived back in town, the calf was up and running around in the back of his truck. It grew up to be part of our herd of milk cows. Strange?

During World War II, I was present two different summers when a group of about five or six men in trucks arrived in Sunnyside. They parked by the barn and arranged with dad to use several of our horses and mules to go into the mountains and canyons.

I watched these taciturn men as they loaded camping equipment and food for the four day trip. My attention was caught by the large lights, and batteries to operate them, they carried. They didn't say much and my questions about their activities were largely ignored.

After they left town, rumors circulated about whether they were communists or merely surveyors. They did have some surveying equipment. Dad passed them off as just government surveyors. He said they would do their surveying and engineering studies by signalling to each other with their lights from the mountain tops.

When they returned several days later, they unloaded the pack horses and mules, put their equipment back in their trucks and departed without saying much. Their actions and speech were typical American, yet remote somehow. Dad had been informed that they were coming and we had the horses and mules, both for packing and riding, available and ready to go. Dad did not express undue concern so who was I to worry about their mission? Yet both times they arrived and departed there was a sense of mystery and secretiveness about them. Strange?

Growing up in Sunnyside I encountered very little that I didn't understand. Yet these happenings still remain strange to me.

THE TIPPLE

In my moving business I spend considerable time on the road. My van does not have a sleeper and, since I enjoy a quiet motel bed over a hard bunk in a noisy rest stop, I stay at motels when I'm on the road. On a recent trip I had finally finished unloading and found myself in Indianapolis about 9 p.m. Finding a newer, mid-priced motel, I asked the clerk at the front desk for my AARP discount and a nice, quiet room at the back of the motel away from the ice machine. The clerk assured me that my room was in the quiet area of the motel away from the parking lot and freeway, and that the ice machine was way down the hall. I retired to my quiet room and after the news I fell asleep.

You'd think that a guy who grew up with humming, rattling and shaking noises fifty yards away from his house twenty-four hours a day, and later, raising nine kids would not be bothered by barely detectable sounds as he drifts off to dreamland. But I am.

The humming started at exactly 2 a.m. I knew the time because the little clock-radio on the nightstand had lighted numbers. I thought that maybe the kitchen was on the floor below and that someone had turned on the garbage disposal. The humming was still going at 3 a.m. I was now wide awake and mad.

I shaved, got dressed and headed to the front desk to check out. The night clerk told me that the soft humming sound was the pool filtering system that turns on each night at 2 a.m. after all the guests have gone to sleep. After expressing my displeasure at the noise and asking for my room fee back (which I didn't get), and getting her apology when I indicated that this would be my first and last stop at this motel, I was off toward the west at 3:45 a.m. regretting some of the words I had uttered to that placating night clerk.

It was just 8 p.m. when I pulled into my favorite motel in Denver, 1,055 miles and sixteen hours later. It was 1C a.m. when the maid, waiting to clean my room, shook my doorknob for the second time. I had slept longer than planned but was soon on my way home to my own bed.

In Sunnyside we lived across the street and creek from the tipple. The tipple was where the coal from the mine was sorted and crushed. The sorting was done on sloped tables called shakers, because that's what they did. After the boney (rocks) were removed, the lumps of coal moved through a series of crushers with giant jaws that reduced the lunch-bucket sized lumps to golf ball size. The shakers and crushers made a steady, continuous racket that I grew up hearing all day and all night, yet I don't remember ever even noticing the noise. Call it age, or hardening of the arteries, or softening of the eardrums, but I would notice that noise today.

With the wind blowing up the canyon before noon and down the canyon after noon, dusting the window sills was one of mother's daily tasks. And the coal dust DID settle at our house. Washing and calcimining the walls and ceilings was a yearly ritual. I don't know if we were bothered by pollen each spring, but we certainly did inhale a lot of coal dust, seemingly without long-lasting negative effects.

After high school, I worked picking boney on the shakers for about six months before college and courting forced me out of full time work. We'd stand by the shakers and pick out the boney from the coal and drop it down a shute into a bin where it was hauled by truck down to the rock pile below town. After going through the crusher, the coal (slack) would go into large bins where it was released into railroad cars for shipment to steel mills elsewhere. Dad worked at the tipple as a railroad car loader.

Above the entrance to the mine was the hoist house. Here a big spool with a long, one-inch steel cable pulled the loaded mine cars up the slope from inside the mine. The spool turned, winding the cable around it as the loaded mine cars were pulled up out of the mine. Bells were used as signals telling the hoist operator when to start winding and when to stop. The steel spool was about six feet by six feet. When the loaded mine cars were out of the mine entrance, tracks were switched and they were on their way to the tipple to be unloaded one at a time, with the empty cars moving forward after being unloaded. When they were all empty, the bells would ring and the hoist operator then pulled them back and returned them to the mine for another load.

One day when I was a kid, I was sitting on the front porch steps of our house when a different noise came from the tipple. As I looked in that direction, empty mine cars were dropping out of the top of the tipple and down three stories to the railroad tracks below. Apparently the wrong signal had been given, or misread, and instead of pulling the empty cars back toward the hoist house, they had been lowered further and when the track ran out they dropped to the ground below. Needless to say, the tipple was shut down and tumult reigned for the rest of the afternoon.

After this event, they curved the tracks at the end, forming a sideways J so that if this mistake happened again, the cars could not get past the curved end of the track. This curve stuck out from the tipple and was visible thereafter.

In the mid-1940s electric mine engines replaced the old cars and hoist house. The steep slope mine entrance was replaced by a gentler slope. The mine car wheels were clamped to the tracks in the tipple and each car rotated to empty it.

When I was about nine years old my friend, Kay Naylor,

and I went to visit his father, Horace Naylor, who was the hoist operator at that time. Horace told us how everything worked and what was happening, thus making us nine year old experts on the hoist and tipple operations.

As the crushed coal and slack was loaded into the railroad cars underneath the tipple, dad and the other loaders would drop (move) the cars a little at a time to get them evenly filled. They would drop them further down the track when they were filled to make room for the next car to be loaded.

The railroad car brakes were activated by turning a metal wheel about the size of a car steering wheel, which in turn was connected to a long steel shaft running down to the gear box and wheels. This brake wheel had to be turned by inserting a stick or rod, about the size of a pick handle, through the wheel and forcing the wheel to turn using the side of the car for leverage. It took great strength and pulling, using body weight, to start and stop the railroad cars. Gravity started the cars moving when the brakes were released.

Our cousin, Wade Turner, worked with dad dropping cars. Wade, a young father of three small children, was working one late shift dropping cars. As he applied the rod to brake the railroad car, the rod broke, sending him under the wheels to the track below. He was crushed under the wheels and died. It was a tragedy that is remembered by surviving Sunnyside coal miners to this day, over forty-five years later.

Dropping cars meant dad and the other loaders had time to spare as the car was loading. They often used this spare time for playful pranks, but that's a story for another chapter.

As a kid, sleeping on the front porch during the summers with the tipple's noisy clatter all night long never bothered me. But if I were to try it now I wouldn't catch a wink no matter how long I stayed in the sack. But maybe that's always the way. We take for granted our surroundings when we're young, never realizing the day will come when even the memories can keep us awake.

Tipple, Shop, Bathhouse and No. 2 Mine (Photo courtesy WM&RM)

Tipple Fire (Photo courtesy WM&RM)

TOWN BOARD MEETINGS

Each fall the election process kicks in and we are exposed to more propaganda than we deserve. Since I've been a candidate for office on several occasions and served on a city council, I wondered about political activities and Town Board meetings in early Sunnyside. So I did some digging through old records.

In 1914 there were 370 registered voters in the unincorporated area of Carbon County known as the Sunnyside Precinct. On the 9th of March 1916, 222 signatures requesting incorporation were presented to the Carbon County Commission. This request was approved on March 11, 1916 and Sunnyside was off and running.

Early copies of Sunnyside Town Board meeting minutes are not available. The first ones I reviewed began January 3, 1939. My father, Taylor W. Turner, was a member of the Town Board at that time and the trustees, as they were called, were paid $2 per month. The mayor got $3. Some of the copies of the minutes are less than a third of a page long. Rarely do any of them take up a full page.

I found that everything that was put in the form of a motion was approved—once by a three to two vote, but it was approved. No discussions are recorded and there is no information indicating how each trustee voted. Excerpts of those nearly sixty year old meetings are most interesting. I am including the original spelling here..

"Jan 3, 1939. It was suggested by Trustee Taylor Turner that a sign be posted to look out for children sleigh riding."

"Jun 5, 1939. The town could spend $544 for asphalt . . . To asphalt the large square in front of the Post Office and go to the Japanese Hotel, and further if Henry Jones could afford to give the asphalt." They needed donated materials and volunteers in those days, too.

"Jul 10, 1939. The mayor instructed the clerk to write to the State Road Commission to complain that the roads haven't been graded for several months." I wonder if the complaint accomplished its purpose. And, if so, if the State Road Commission was thanked. There's no more about this.

"Aug 7, 1939. Moved that Francis Dennison, Henry Jones and Orson Turner be appointed to fill vacancies caused by death, resignation or removal or otherwise on the town council of Sunnyside." Were they appointed? And what would be cause for removal from the council? No answers found to these questions.

"Oct 2, 1939. Tony Ledger suggested that the town set a side [sic] the back street for sleigh riding. . . Also the street be graded and fix a hill by the school for sleigh riding. Approved."

"Apr 1, 1940. Moved that Henry Jones be paid $79 for cleaning the town. Approved."

"Jun 3, 1940. Moved to buy a tennis net for the town tennis court. Approved."

"Sep 2, 1940. Taylor Turner moved the town hire Jack Patterson Sr to chop weeds and burs [sic] from town street in lower town. Approved."

"Nov 4, 1940. Taylor Turner asked the town to get culverts along road in lower town. Passed."

"Jan 6, 1941. Taylor Turner excused on account of sickness." In the eight years of minutes I read, this is the only meeting I can find that dad missed.

During some of the meetings, the town clerk presented the town bank balance. It appears that cash flow problems never change. On April 7, 1941 the bank balance was $570.70. On July 1, 1941 it was $453.96. On August 4, 1941 it was down to $420.78.

The highlight of some of the meetings seemed to be approving the checks to be written. Some months this was for four or five checks in addition to showing the amount of the checks for the mayor and trustees. Other months the total went as high as twelve checks to be paid.

With the war in Europe expanding and apparent concern for defense facilities, including coal mines, the town minutes reflect this concern and support for strong defense.

"Jul 21, 1941. Special Session. National Defense was taken up. Drive for Aluminum committee appointed: Archie Morrison, Henry Jones, J.L. Durrant, Tony Ledger, Horace Naylor, Dantey [sic] Pederiva, Taylor Turner, Fred Flaim, J.E. Peacock, Davy Menotti."

"Aug 4, 1941. Taylor Turner motioned to order two deputy city marshals badges for $3.25. Approved."

"Oct 6, 1941. Election judges appointed: Mrs. F.E. Dennison, Ella Turner, Doris Lindsey. James Peacock appointed 'Defense Coordinator' for Sunnyside."

These next two items in two different meetings are interesting. Although how they voted is not recorded, when they made a motion and seconded the motion, it was recorded. Two members of this board were in the Bishopric of the Sunnyside L.D.S. Ward.

Continuing with the October 6, 1941 minutes, "James Peacock moved to -remove slot machines from town. Taylor Turner seconded. Motion passed."

"Nov 3, 1941. The slot machine problem was presented. Motion made to reestablish the slot machine in Sunnyside. Vote: Yes 3, No 2."

"Dec 1, 1941. Motion to give Sunnyside Christmas Celebration $10. Approved."

"Jan 5, 1942. The town marshals will attend public dances."

The minutes for the following month indicate that, perhaps, the town marshals was not happy with his additional duties and the board took care of his concerns. "Feb 2, 1942. Town marshals to be paid $2 for each public dance he is directed to protect in addition to his $3 salary. The mayor asked the council to clean out old Celar [sic] by the depot to store waist [sic] supplies for defense."

"Mar 2, 1942. Treasurers report is $103.94."

"Apr 7, 1942. Treasurers report is $50.65." This is the lowest balance on hand reflected in any of the minutes. With the war machine and economy now gearing up for the long road ahead, things could only get better. And they did.

"Jun 1, 1942. Treasurers report is $634.45."

"Sep 7, 1942. Moved, the board approve the addition of Sunny Dale subdivision. Approved."

"May 3, 1943. Deputy Sheriff ordered to have all slot machines removed from confectionary excluding the music machine. Motion by Taylor Turner that town purchase blankets for the jail." This time the slot machines were gone for good.

Up until this time, power for Sunnyside had been furnished by eighteen steam boilers which were fueled and maintained by the Utah Fuel Mining Company. Each household paid $1 per month for electricity and $1 per month for water. Electricity for the houses had been turned off part of each day. Then things changed.

"Jun 9, 1943. Franchise granted to Utah Power and Light Co."

"Jul 9, 1943. Frank Ellis appointed town marshals."

"Aug 2, 1943. New ordinance approved regulating garbage." This new ordinance was not explained.

Routine business was noted in the minutes for the next year and a half. Then on June 29, 1945, Mayor Horace

Naylor resigned as he was leaving town to operate his own business. Taylor Turner was appointed acting mayor.

In the January 1946 meeting, "Mayors salary $6, board members $4."

At the meeting the following month, "Mayors salary $14, board members $8." This raise is an indication of how the war had increased Sunnyside's economic base.

In the December 1947 minutes Francis E. Dennison is listed as the mayor of Sunnyside. After serving sixteen years on the Sunnyside Town Board, two of them as mayor, and concurrently serving fifteen years on the Sunnyside Welfare Board and thirteen years on the Carbon County School Board, Dad went on to serve four years on the Carbon County Commission. He was a good example of what service, not just politics, should be.

The power plant crew in 1900. (Photo courtesy WM&RM)

We can only speculate about the woman in the photo. Was she the boss?
The first women's libber? Working the shift for her husband? Whatever
she's accusing them of, they're not buying into it. (Just a guess)

The First Sunnyside Power Plant.
(Photo courtesy WM&RM)

The 1902 Power Plant. (Photo courtesy GEA-HBLL-BYU)

TRAINS

One of the very special experiences I had while growing up in Sunnyside was living fifty yards from the railroad tracks, switching areas and the tipple that processed the coal as it came out of the mine. From the steps on our front porch, I had daily contact with a living Railroad Museum.

In mankind's quest for ultimate technology and maximum economic benefit, some great and wonderful things have been left behind. For example, that giant, smoke belching, metal dinosaur that tied America's East and West—the Railroad Steam Engine.

From the ringside seat on our front steps I could see it all. There were four sets of tracks. The engine always faced north, or up the canyon. It never turned around in that part of town, instead always backing down the tracks when it had completed whatever job was required of it.

There were three switches to get the engine and empty cars onto the other tracks. I liked to call them the Three Skinny One-Armed Switch Sisters. All they ever asked from the engine crew was to be turned a quarter of a turn so they could smile at each other every other day. The engine crew filled their needs and the sisters remained happy. When it was time to get the railroad cars onto another track, the railroad man would give a one-armed sister a handshake and turn her toward her sisters. At least that's how I imagined it from my vantage point on the front steps as I watched them switch tracks.

The four sets of tracks across the road between the depot and the tipple ran by and under the tipple. One was the main line and the other three were used for loading the coal cars.

The tracks merged into two sets of tracks north of the

depot. The switch sister on that side of the depot could not see one sister when she turned, but the other sister said that she was happy, so who was I to argue? The depot was where freight was unloaded. No passenger trains ever came into Sunnyside, just coal and freight trains. There was an apartment in the upstairs section of the depot where the depot manager and his family lived. The ice cellar was west of the depot.

Just southwest of the depot was a little shed where the railroad maintenance car was located. When it was time for the maintenance crew to change railroad ties or clean up around the tracks, they would move the little car out at a right angle to the main tracks then, with everyone lifting a corner at the same time, they would set the maintenance car on the tracks and leave for their work duties. Movies of the Old West show a "pumper" car with handles to pump to make it move, but someone older than me will have to tell about that item. The maintenance car I saw had a motor that made it move under its own power.

Historians mention the crew of an engine as being the engineer, the fireman and the brakeman. Maybe that's the way it worked in other trains, but all I ever saw were two men in the cab, who often waved when they saw some of us kids watching. And from the front steps I did see once, and wave at, a man in the caboose as he watched the world go by with smoke-filled eyes.

You don't see a caboose much anymore, except at railroad museums. The caboose was the last car on the train and it was where the crew members who were not on duty sat, ate or slept while waiting their turn in the cab of the engine. One of the engineers once let me look inside a caboose when it was parked by the depot. It had an eating and sleeping area, and an upstairs room on the back where there was a seat on either side and a sliding window to wave from.

When the big, black giant came to town, it was usually pulling a string of empty coal cars that had to be divided up and put on three of the sets of tracks. The stationary, white crossbars with black letters "railroad crossing" written on them warned motorists and pedestrians alike to watch for trains or, if you were waiting to cross, there would be a short wait while the train did its thing. A few years later, red flashing lights warning of incoming trains were added.

After hooking up a string of coal filled cars in the proper location, the engine would need to get started on a slight incline. With a pull of the throttle, the big wheels would spin as the train started slowly moving. After dark you could see the sparks fly as the wheels spun. In later years, as a teenage driver on slick roads, my car would start out the same way. However, the driver of the train didn't get to experience the fish-tailing that I did.

Each coupling session would last about an hour to get all of the cars positioned on the track and then to wave at the engineer as he backed down the tracks past the tipple. A couple of days later we would do it all again.

As the train cars coupled with the parked cars there would be a great clanging of metal and whistling as the air hoses were released. Each engine had a bell that would ring. I never did understand why the bell rang but, with clanging, whistling, ringing and smoke and steam billowing from the engine as it moved along the tracks, it was a sight, sound and smell never to be forgotten.

I remember when the first diesel engine brought a string of coal cars into town. It was a new experience but could never replace the spectacle of the old giant metal dinosaurs. On our trips to Provo we often saw as many as four diesel engines at a time helping pull a string of loaded coal cars up over the top of Soldier Summit.

Clair tells about the time he was riding home from Price on the school bus when he and a buddy noticed a slow train moving up the tracks toward Sunnyside pulling a string of empty coal cars. The two high schoolers talked the bus driver into letting them off the bus to catch the train. The driver did and Clair and his buddy ran alongside the tracks, grabbed onto a ladder on the outside of a coal car and clambered over the top and inside. It was cold and dirty and bumpy in the car and took much longer to get to Sunnyside than the school bus did. He got home half-frozen and covered with coal dust. Dad and mother didn't say much to him. They knew that the ride in that dirty, slow, cold railroad car was punishment enough.

After high school, and before he went into the army, Clair and a friend decided to hitchhike (thumb a ride) to Grand Junction, Colorado. They got a ride to Green River but weren't able to catch another ride there. They spotted a slow-moving train headed in the direction of Grand Junction so ran along the railroad tracks again and hoisted themselves into an empty boxcar. They discovered that this was another one of those "the fun is not worth the trouble rides. They arrived in Grand Junction cold and tired with smoke-filled eyes. After a night on the town, they hitchhiked back to Sunnyside, riding in the comfort of automobiles all the way.

My one and only train ride (other than the ski train from Price to Schofield and back in high school), happened a month after I got married and was in the Air Force. I was to report to Camp Kilmer in New Jersey. I knew nothing about pullman or dining cars. With my loaded duffle bag in hand I boarded the train in Price and began the three days and nights journey.

I slept on my seat and ate sandwiches from the vending machine. I was afraid to ask questions and assumed that this was how all train passengers traveled. After two days and nights the train arrived in Chicago. The Chicago train station looked bigger than the entire town of Sunnyside. The train for New Jersey left on track eighteen. After a hot bowl of soup at the lunch counter in the station I was off again, arriving in New Jersey twenty-four hours later.

As I rode I was reminded of the time a few years earlier when I just about got an unexpected train ride. Several of us were in Johnny Preston's 1936 Chev at the top of the Columbia dugway. It was night and the train was coming. Someone said, "Hit it! I think we can beat it!" I was sitting in the back seat, right side. As we crossed the tracks, I could make out every bar on the engine's cow catcher, and the train headlight lit up the car brighter than the noonday sun. Four pale faced boys finished the trip to Columbia in silence. If life's dumb events are recorded on video to show in heaven, this ride would surely be included. And, speaking of heaven, I hope that at least one of those old steam engines will be resurrected so my grandkids will get to see and enjoy one as I did as a child.

In my travels over the superhighways of America, I sometimes end up in a motel in a town with a train station. Sometimes just as I'm dozing off, I'll hear that familiar train whistle in the distance. Instantly I'm back in Sunnyside on the front porch steps once more. What a way to go to sleep.

WHEELS

I read in the paper recently that many large cities are outlawing "in-line" skating on public sidewalks or parking lots. I've watched some of those "in-line" skaters. They can really get up to speed. With the row of wheels on the bottom of their skates they can beat anything we used to do when I was a boy in Sunnyside.

The first wheels I remember were those under the buggy that mother pushed. I was the passenger until little brother Grant came along and replaced me. Thinking about that buggy reminds me of a joke: "What's worse than a dog with fleas?" "A horse with a buggy behind." Now, back to the memories.

After the buggy came the tricycle. Grant and I got matching tricycles for Christmas when I was about five years old. Max Durrant came by and wanted to ride one of them so I loaned him mine and borrowed Grant's and we rode them to lower town and back.

Then in the growing evolution, roller skates were next. We had the kind that strapped to your shoes. They were metal, including the wheels, and adjustable. There was a clamp on the front and a leather strap across your instep. A skate key tightened the clamp to the soles of your shoes. With worn shoes and a tight clamp you could get kinked toes.

There were times when a bad ride and a tight clamp pulled the soles right off our shoes. Dad wasn't enthusiastic about roller skates that clamped on. He preferred winter and the new shoe ice skates for us kids. He didn't have to worry about mending our shoe soles with them.

The sidewalks in Sunnyside were cracked and broken all

over town. There were very few places where we could find three slabs of unbroken cement in a row, so skating in either direction from our house was hazardous to our health. But, like poverty, it was something we all lived with. We knew dad wasn't going to take us to Price just to roller skate on the smooth sidewalks there, so we learned to dodge and jump the cracks and broken slabs.

When the skates were broken beyond repair, we made wooden scooters from the wheels and pieces of lumber we scrounged. The scooters were a little more stable than skates, with the upright 2x4 pole and handle to hang on to. But we still had to be alert riding on those damaged sidewalks or we'd end up rubbing sore knees and elbows.

Next in our evolutionary process came bikes and go-carts. Go-carts were made from used lumber and metal wheelbarrow or discarded buggy wheels. Our go-cart brakes were a piece of wood pushed against a fast spinning rear wheel. Listening to one of those vehicles coming down the cracked, broken and, in some places missing, sidewalks with three or four happy, yelling kids was worse than hearing a runaway eighteen-wheeler on Wolf Creek Pass. Somehow we made it through this phase of growing up with only bruises, cuts and concrete burns.

If I had known that learning to ride a bicycle so young meant being ready to deliver milk, I would have delayed this process awhile longer. But, once Clair taught me the finer points of bicycle riding after giving me the first lesson while we were on a break from cleaning the church, it was too late to change my mind. It was only a short time until I was an accomplished bike rider and began delivering milk. Early on, dad got on my case when I wrecked with a rack of loaded milk bottles on the handlebars. I was much more careful after that. Riding with racks of full bottles of milk took skill, balance and endurance on our one-speed bikes. And once we got really good at it, Grant and I got to deliver papers on our bikes, too. This phase of growing up lasted a few more years before I graduated to real wheels—CARS.

As a senior citizen with nine grown children and thirty plus grandchildren, I appreciate my parents more than ever. In those days, at age fifteen and a half there was no driver training class. We learned by trial and error, sometimes lots of error. If we ever go back to the old days for driver training, I'd recommend that you young people stay close to your mother. Dads are great at dispensing flak and mothers are slow to condemn errors. If you have a choice, learn to drive under your mother's direction. You'll grow up with less stress to cause problems in your old age.

The rule in the 1940s was that two weeks before your sixteenth birthday you got a learner's permit. With this permit, you could now get behind the steering wheel if you had a licensed driver in the passenger seat. I know that learner's permits are issued these days but that's only after a term of Driver Education. Our driver education was watching other drivers and taking over whenever they'd let us. And there were no automatic transmissions then so learning to shift gears and pump the clutch was a real car jerker.

The eye exam as part of the licensing process indicated that I was to wear glasses while driving. I hated glasses, but loved driving, so I got the glasses. Things were a little sharper with the glasses and I started seeing things I hadn't seen before, but it would be another four years before I was wearing them permanently.

Dad had a "Grandfather License" which was given in the days before tests were given and was supposed to last a lifetime. It nearly did for him. He was in his seventies before the rules changed and he had to take a driver's test and get an up-to-date license. His driving left something to be desired sometimes. He would not shift to a lower gear until it was absolutely necessary. I swear I could hear the motor calling for a lower gear on several occasions when he was driving. He always held his hands in the two and ten o'clock positions on the steering wheel. He would let the wheel slide through his hands on a turn. We always did slow turns with dad at the wheel. As a teenager, I had lots of answers. I told him to let his hands move around with the wheel for faster turns, but I was ignored.

When Grant got his license, too, we went together and bought a "love knob" and put it on the steering wheel of the family sedan. This, later to be outlawed, device looked like a doorknob and was placed on a right angle on one of the spokes of the steering wheel. It was supposed to be for fast turning but got it's nickname because when you had one of these on your steering wheel and your girl beside you, you didn't need both hands on the steering wheel. It was a status symbol. All the young drivers had one. Dad never did approve of it and one Sunday when he got his long sleeved shirt caught on the "love knob," Grant and I got the message that it was to be removed as soon as church was over. In the interest of driver and teenage safety, it was promptly removed.

We parked our cars in the area behind our house which required two turns on a slight incline. While I was still learning to drive, I had a tough time coordinating the clutch and a lower gear. In other words, I did not like to shift down. When I was driving, I would try to get a 'run' up our alley so the momentum would carry me to the parking spot. This meant cornering on two wheels at thirty miles per hour. Mother would tolerate this but one trip when dad was in the passenger seat, he insisted that I was to shift down if I was to continue driving his car. I got the message.

At age seventeen, using my earnings from a summer janitor job at B.Y.U. and negotiating favorable financial terms from Grant and mother, I had enough money to purchase a $125 Model A Ford. Two years later dad and I signed a note at the bank in Price for $500 and I drove off in a 1939 Chev Coupe from a car dealership in Price. I now had more friends and less money than I ever thought possible.

I learned that a car would run better if you removed the muffler and painted the tires white. So I did both. The straight pipe in place of the muffler made a loud, pleasing sound to my young ears. Old people just don't seem to understand that noise and enjoyment are synonymous. I've finally lived long enough to understand why old people feel the way they do.

White sidewalls became the rage. We couldn't afford white sidewall tires so we painted them on. We're not talking about today's one inch strip on a tire. We painted from rim to tread, and repainted when they got scuffed.

There were no turn signals on cars in those days. With the left arm out the window, the arm bent up meant a right turn; the arm straight out meant a left turn and the arm turned down meant slowing down and, perhaps, stopping. You can imagine what the inside of the car and your arm felt like in the cold winter months. I remember helping install the first turn signal on the car steering column with a friend in 1950. By the time I got out of the Air Force in 1955, they were factory installed and standard equipment on all new cars.

After World War II in 1946, our cousin came by our house in a new Chev Coupe, the first time in four years that new cars were again available. I can still see the hood ornament. It looked like the top half of an H and was about four inches square.

In 1950 dad traded his 1938 stake truck for a newer, used

pickup. We still had the old 1937 Chev family sedan and Grant had purchased a classy 1937 Chev Coupe from our cousin Phillip. We were loaded with wheels, something unheard of ten years earlier.

Dad lived long enough to own a car with an automatic transmission. I believe when that happened all the engines in Detroit gave a collective sigh of relief that none of them would ever again be subjected to driving in third gear too long.

WINTER

It was snowing hard when my granddaughters kicked the snow off their summer shoes and came in after school for something to eat. "Where are your galoshes?" I blurted out, and before they could answer, "and why are you just wearing anklets?"

Without responding they headed straight for the fridge and popped a plate full of corn dogs and burritos in the microwave. As they waited for the buzzer one of them said, "I wonder if Gramps learned those new words as he crossed the plains?"

In this high-tech, virtual reality, couch potato world, I worry about grandkids. In Sunnyside when I was a boy and it snowed, that's when we headed out of the house. That's when the fun began.

With a sled, a slick road and a good run, you could ride on your sled from the hospital across the street from the house where I was born to down in front of Peacock's house. The road leveled out slightly from there to Lizzy Jones's place then started its downward angle again. In front of the store, main street made a sharp right turn and became quite steep. It leveled out again crossing the railroad tracks and over the bridge. Past the bridge the road made another sharp turn to the left and was downhill past our place and clear to the end of lower town.

We all wished that the D-8 Cat operator who did the original grading of main street would have lowered his blade and made a cut where the road went past the amusement hall lawn, making it slope down. If he had done this, we could have hit our sleds on a full run and, if we could have navigated the two sharp turns and not met a car on the bridge, we would have ridden clear to Davy Menotti's store three miles below town.

Another thing we did in the winter was biz. I can't even find this word in the dictionary, but I know we did it. The closest word I can find is "bizarre," which means odd or extravagant. That describes it.

Here's how it worked: When the snows came, you would join your friends and watch for a slow moving car headed in your direction. Just as it got abreast of you, you would grab the back bumper, squat down, and slide on your shoes. It was great fun.

The turn in front of our house and the one in front of the store were favorite 'catching on' places because cars had to slow for the turn and then it was uphill. Sometimes it was so slick we would have to help push the car to get it going first, then it was easy to hang on. Some of the older women drivers got mad at us. Sometimes they even stopped and yelled for us to "get away from there!" Young women drivers were too scared to stop once we hooked on.

Billy Preston, my cousin Phillip and my brother Clair would give us the best rides. They would pull us through deep snow when they could find some. Phillip would also let us hook a string of sleds behind his car. The last sled would really whip.

When bizzing, there were several hazards. One was the bare spots in the road. If you hit a bare spot, your feet went out from under you. I believe the term for that was "drugged." Even the meaning of the word has changed over the years. This happened to my younger brother Grant once and it "drugged" off all of his coat buttons. Mother was not happy.

Another hazard was the two sets of railroad tracks. When you got to these it was heads up, or wham! Martin Rodosh got his leg seriously twisted once when he hit the tracks wrong.

Today's cars would have been bad news in those bygone days. Modern bumpers have no space between them and the back of the car. Old bumpers had space and they were curved and great for hanging on. All of the old cars had the exhaust pipe coming out of the back. The last guy to catch on got the exhaust pipe since that was the only place left, and since his lungs were not already full of carbon monoxide.

Another hazard when bizzing was created by one of our own bizzers. I don't remember who started it, but here's how it worked: When we had a bumper full of kids and everyone was having fun, the kid on the outside would give a quick push sideways with his inside foot, shoving the feet out from under everyone else. The domino effect. Now everyone, except one, was dragging on their bellies and trying to get their feet under them again. And, with practice, most of us accomplished this. From then on we had to watch out for tricks from the outside guys.

We never had an ice skating rink in Sunnyside, but who needed one? We had the creek that flowed through town. A part of it broke off and made a shallow pool down by the Junction. This froze over every winter. It wasn't smooth but it made for challenging ice skating. If you could stay on your feet on this patch of ice, you could stay on your feet anywhere. And some nights the road down through town was a solid sheet of ice and we could put on our skates and skate out in the road from the top of town all the way to the end of lower town.

All the kids in Sunnyside looked forward to winter. My parents were not all that crazy about it, especially if my dad had to drive in it. When the car slid around, or got stuck, mother always wished we children were somewhere else or, at least, that we had our toques pulled down tighter over our ears because that's when dad began to quote scriptures. Toque (pronounced 'toke'—a knitted cap covering the head), that's another word we don't hear in the same context anymore.

When a town is in the canyon, winter lasts longer. We didn't see many snowplows until we got closer to Price. In Sunnyside, we just waited for that great snow shovel in the sky.

As my granddaughters finished their half eaten meals, I wished that someone would invent a gizmo that cou d put unused catsup back in the bottle. After watching my grandkids, I suggest that the Old Mother Hubbard rhyme be changed to 'Old Grandmother Hubbard,' because I now know why her cupboard was bare.

As my granddaughters walked past me toward the door, one of them said, "Gramps, you're about out of corn dogs and burritos." Today's kids may not be as smart as we were, but they are a heck of a lot brighter.

But sometimes I wonder if they're not missing out on something. Then again, they just don't make winters like they used to in Sunnyside.

WORLD WAR II

My generation is the last generation to date to witness forthright victory as the ultimate military goal. Too many times since 1946 we have seen our country's young soldiers die in foreign lands under United Nations Commands. Whether they've been called Conflict" or "Police Action" or "Containment" or any other names, they've still been wars. "The War to End All Wars" in 1918 didn't end all wars, it was just the beginning of the end of our policy of calling them wars when they were fought for political expediency. Historians disagree on the exact date of the beginning of World War II. Some even regard WWI and WWII as parts of the same war with only a breathing spell in between.

My knowledge of World War I was only what I read in history books but I was ten years old when World War II began for the United States with the bombing of Pearl Harbor on 7 December 1941. Two events are embedded in my memory of this date these fifty-five years later. The first was that two days earlier Winifred had received a letter dated December 1st from her Air Force husband, Michael, who was on a troop ship in Pearl Harbor waiting for transport out; and the second event was that the nisei (American-born Japanese) children in Sunnyside didn't come to school the next day. But the following day, Tuesday, when they showed up, the class bully was extremely verbally abusive to them, especially my good friends Henry, Harry and Harold Nitsuma. He made it sound like they were personally responsible for the bombing that Sunday.

This was the first example of prejudice I had experienced and it has been a constant reminder throughout my life that guilt by association or, in this case, nationality is never fair or just. Color, national origin or religion should never be used as an excuse for cruelty. But this example, in retrospect helps explain, to our national shame, why it wasn't long before American citizens of Japanese descent all along the Pacific Coast were sent to relocation camps in Colorado, Utah and other states.

I was fourteen years old when the Allies achieved victory over Germany in May 1945 and over Japan the following August. Although the Nitsuma family were not sent to a relocation camp because their father, Charles, was a coal miner and coal was needed in the war effort, by a strange quirk of fate he was killed, along with twenty-two other miners, in a mine explosion the day after V. E. (Victory in Europe) Day.

Those war years were a challenging time to be growing up in our little multi-ethnic coal mining town. Nearly all able-bodied young men in Sunnyside left for the various military services in the early 1940s. Families of servicemen hung framed stars in the windows of their houses indicating how many of their sons or daughters were serving their country. Many houses in Sunnyside had stars hanging in their windows. Early in the war James Patterson, Ned's age, was taken prisoner by the Japanese and spent nearly four years in often inhumane confinement. Ella Ruth's friend, Garth Williams, was killed during the Allied D-Day Invasion of the Normandy coast on June 6, 1944.

During World War II when servicemen came home on furlough they proudly wore their uniforms to church, dances and other public events, and the entire community respected and admired them. Sunnyside and the whole country were united in the goal of victory. We all were filled with patriotism, the flag was flown proudly and "God Bless America" and "The Star Spangled Banner" were sung fervently at public gatherings and meetings.

To aid in the war effort, the coal mines and coke ovens were put in full production. Additional miners and laborers arrived in town steadily and soon two new communities, Sunnydale and Dragerton, were built below town. Three bunkhouses were constructed in Sunnyside to house all the additional essential workers.

Rationing began soon after the start of the war because urgent requirements for war materials caused many shortages in consumer goods. Sugar, gasoline, rubber products and shoes were some of the things I remember being rationed. The purchase of War Bonds and Savings Stamps was promoted. We took twenty-five cents a week to school to buy a savings stamp to put in our Savings Book. The book held $18.25 worth of stamps. When it was filled it was traded for a War Bond that would bring $25 when it matured in ten years. Workers purchased War Bonds with part of their paychecks each month.

In school, in addition to the savings stamps, we became part of a group called "The Write A Fighter Corps." The goal was for each of us to write to a service person at least monthly. We were also given cards and learned to identify military airplanes. My favorites were the P-38 and the P-51. The war movies that were shown at the theater nearly always had several scenes showing B-25 bombers, which we readily identified.

Also at this time, Grant and I and our friends formed a "Commando Club" and staged mock battles on the hillsides around town. Sometimes in the evening after Grant and I had spent hours playing commandos, mother would quietly sing a very old song. As I listened to the words then I thought it was a wonderful war song. Now when I think of it, I hear the pathos and don't think it glorifies war after all, but does the opposite. I'm not sure I remember all the words right and I have no idea who wrote it but it went something like this:

Two little boys had two little toys,
each had a wooden horse.
Gaily they played, each summer's day,
warriors both, of course.
One little chap, he had a mishap
broke off his horse's head.
Cried for his toy, then cried for joy,
when his brave comrade said,
"Do you think I could leave you crying
"when there's room on my horse for two?
"Climb up here Jack, don't be sighing,
"it'll go just as fast with two.
"When we grow up we'll be soldiers
"and our horses will not be toys.
"Do you think that we will remember
"when we were two little boys?"

Long years passed and war came at last.
Gaily they marched away.
Cannons roared loud, mid the mad crowd
wounded and dying Jack lay.
Out came a cry as a horse rushed by,
out from the ranks of the blue
Galloped away to where Jack lay,
came a voice strong and true,
"Do you think I could leave you dying
"when there's room on my horse for two?
"Climb up here Jack don't be sighing,
"it'll go just as well with two.
"Say Jack, I'm all in a tremble—-
"it might be the battle noise—
"But it might be that I remember
"when we were two little boys."

Sales tax began during the war. It began as a quarter of a cent on a dollar. Plastic tax tokens worth this amount became available. It wasn't long before the tax and tokens were raised to a half cent on a dollar. Pennies from 1942 to 1944 were made of lead because copper was needed for the war effort. Also for the war effort, families collected scrap iron and aluminum. Our family collected both. I remember taking the aluminum foil from gum and candy bar wrappers and adding them to our aluminum ball at home. Each ball grew to be bigger than a softball by the time we turned it in.

The war contributed greatly to the rise of patriotic songs. Juke boxes at the confectionery and cafes in Price and Provo played "Over There," "It's a Long, Long Way to Tipperary," Upkeep the Home Fires Burning," and "Till we Meet Again," songs of One that our parents had sung. As the war continued, "Love Letters," "We'll Meet Again," "I'll Be Seeing You," "It's Been a Long, Long Timers and other new songs with military separation themes were added. We sang along with, and danced to, them all.

There were no new cars available between 1942 and 1945 because plants and assembly lines were producing military machines and equipment. Women joined the work force in record numbers, replacing men who had gone to war. Hollywood stars entered the military service and many of them attended War Bond Rallies -and entertained the troops overseas or at U.S.O. clubs. Movies depicted war and hero themes and short newsreels showing military activities around the world were added to the feature film at theaters.

President Franklin D. Roosevelt and United Mine Workers President, John L. Lewis, were heroes along with those in military service. Dean had completed training and received his pilot's license in the years just before the war so he was assigned to Texas to teach new recruits how to fly. After completing high school, Clair was drafted into the army.

Early in the war, the government created an Office of Censorship to censor all communications between the United States and other countries. A serviceman overseas could not write about anything that might jeopardize national security, including the location of the troops. We knew that Clair had been sent overseas but didn't know where. His letters would sometimes arrive with words and sentences cut out by the censors. But he outsmarted the military's best. Mother's name was Ella L. Turner. After she had written to Clair saying that some of his letters were censored, his next letter arrived addressed to Ella L. Turner. Then the following letter arrived addressed to Ella E. Turner. I remember mother saying just before she opened it, "I wonder why he put E?" The next letter from Clair was a dead giveaway that he was trying to tell us something because it was addressed to Ella Y. Turner. She, and we, knew now he was telling us something but we didn't know what it was until the next two letters arrived addressed to Ella T. and Ella E. Mother put them all together and we knew Clair was in Leyte in the Philippine Islands. We children were sworn to secrecy so we wouldn't hinder the war effort.

In the meantime, after nearly six weeks, Winifred finally heard from Michael. The ship he had been on was the last ship to leave Pearl Harbor before it was bombed. It was even later that she learned he and his air crew had been heavily involved in the terrible battles with Rommel's Afrika Korps in North Africa.

During the summers of these war years, Grant and I worked picking fruit on the Orem Bench while staying in Provo. One summer we worked alongside a group of German prisoners of war, picking cherries and peaches. A guard tower can still be seen at the corner of 8th North and 8th East where Mr. Stratton's orchards were located. The guarding soldiers carried rifles but no bullets. When we asked why, they said the prisoners could not speak English and had no place to run and, besides, they were earning American dollars picking fruit. The prisoners were very friendly and we sometimes exchanged a few words with them and learned a few new ones from them.

Finally the war ended in clear-cut victories for the Allies. And we on the home front were praised for helping win World War II. We did not suffer hardships comparable to those in the fighting forces or of the people in the war-torn areas. But, as a united and unified nation, we provided the tools that gave the Allies victory.

We seem to have lost that national patriotic unification in the years since then. And part of that loss can be attributed to fuzzy political thinking and muddy national goals. It's no wonder so many of our young people seem to have no clear-cut goals or dreams for the future. I have to agree with General MacArthur when he said, "There can be no substitute for victory."

A special occation during WW II was when Commander Jack Dempsey came to Sunnyside promoting the sale of War Bonds.
(Photo courtesy Lynn Turnbull Butler)

Wisdom And
The Big Picture

As I get closer to the time when my sojourn on this earth is over, I realize that in my endeavor to gain wisdom almost everyone who became part of my life has had something positive to offer. The old adage that "when the student is ready, the teacher will appear" applies to me today as never before.

Over the years I have learned that most people behave just as they are supposed to behave. I've also learned that we don't ever change someone else, although too many of us spend a lifetime trying. Those who have mastered the "unconditional lovers injunction we were given, understand the big picture. My grandmother was one of those people.

Grandmother Larsen stayed with us in Sunnyside many times. She had faith like no one I've ever met. If she said something, it was true. As an example, one of the times she was with us I cut my arm and it was not healing as it should. She invited me to go with her to gather pine gum from the pinon trees on the mountain behind our house. All I knew about pine gum was that it was just sticky sap. Grandma collected some in a jar. When we got home, she made a poultice out of warm water and the pine gum. She put it on my arm, wrapping gauze around it and pronounced that in two days we'd take the gauze off and the sore would be just about healed. We did and it was. Grandma was like that. She lived by faith and the wisdom of the ages.

Shortly after Grant and I got cars of our own, our two, along with the old family Chev, took all of the parking space by the back of the house. Dad had to park his truck by the barn. One morning I was in a hurry to get started for school in Price. I made a wide half circle backward, as I had always done, to face the street and head toward Price. Halfway into the backward turn there was a "thud" and as I looked out the rear window I realized I had backed into dad's truck. His bumper caved in my trunk lid. Dad heard the noise and came out of the house. In angry tones I asked him why he parked his truck right where we turned around. He replied that we had taken all the closer places. Then he offered some words of wisdom, "If you don't look where you are going it won't matter where I park, there's a good chance you'll do it again." He was right.

I've learned that there are many things we stew and fuss about that don't matter at all. I thought about the wisdom and 'the big picture' dad and grandma and so many others imparted to me as I grew up in Sunnyside when recently I stopped to help a friend of mine who had just discovered that his car had a flat tire. When I arrived he was kicking the guilty tire and ranting about being late and all the things he had to do. I thought about dad and his "if you don't look where you are going" advice as I watched my friend's stress level rising.

Calmly I said to the angry man, "Consider yourself lucky. A flat tire is small stuff compared to having a stroke from high blood pressure. If you stop and think about the big picture, you'll realize that fixing this tire will take less time than cursing it. Come on, let's get the tire changed." His breathing slowed and I could see his body begin to relax as he silently nodded and lifted his jack out of the trunk of his car.

Many times in the last few years I've thought about the absence of stress I enjoyed while growing up in Sunnyside. Everything and everyone in town then traveled at a slower pace. We all kept busy at work or play, but there wasn't the hectic pace I see so often now. Sunnyside was a great place to live and a great place to grow up.

I'd like to think that the Sunnyside I knew as a boy will somehow rise again to its glory days with miners, horses and cows, fun and games, picnics in the canyons, activities in the school gym and all of those wonderful things I enjoyed. But I know that's my memories talking.

The old town is completely gone and the name has been given to that subdivision called Sunnydale that rose from the dust during the 1940s. Some of the old timers stayed there after retiring but they, too, are getting old and the new people moving in will only get part of the story of the Sunnyside I knew.

I've often wondered what event caused Sunnyside to fade away. Did it begin when the depression hit in the 1930s and no one had money to purchase coal and some of the houses near the asphalt mill were sold? (Our family bought two and used the materials to build a new home in Provo.) Did it begin later when World War II ended and military hardware production was no longer necessary? Or was it, perhaps, the mine explosion in 1945 that dampened so many spirits?

Then again, maybe Sunnyside's decline started when paved roads became more economical to do on the spot than have the asphalt shipped in. Or did the dear old town begin to die when the school was moved to Dragerton, another World War II boom town, or when the Post Office, mine office and store relocated to Sunnydale?

The decline could have started when Geneva Steel Company in Orem put in a modern coke making section, forcing the old beehive style ovens to close forever. Or, perhaps, the environmental movement and the need for cleaner fuel played a large part in Sunnyside's demise.

Whatever it was, the Sunnyside I knew as a boy is gone forever. Or is it? The houses are gone, as is the barn, the school house, the tipple, the bathhouse, the amusement hall, the tennis court, the depot, the store and the post office. But the memories those of us who lived there have are as vivid and enduring as though Sunnyside was still alive.

Not long ago, I returned to the place of my birth to sit on the mountainside above where our old house used to be. It was a pleasant, quiet afternoon as I watched the sinking sun move shadows up the mountain and ledges behind where the amusement hall once stood. I noticed that the breeze still blows up the canyon and swirls of coal dust still rise out of the area where the tipple once stood in all its majesty.

I was mentally playing another game of tennis on the old tennis court when I saw movement on the hillside between where the lamp house and the store were once located. In a moment, four fully-grown Big Horn sheep appeared and walked slowly, feeding as they went, along that trail. I knew then why I had given up hunting as I had known it in my younger years. It was beautiful to watch the sheep graze, peaceful and unafraid. It was a scene I'll treasure the rest of my days.

As I sat watching the sheep, I felt a breath of air drift near and felt someone settle down on the boulder beside me. I turned and smiled and asked, "What do you think of it now?"

With a slight nasal twang he answered slowly, "It looks just about like it did when I arrived here a hundred years ago. My three sons and I began working a seam of coal just across the way and down a little. We saw lots of wild sheep and deer in those days. We even saw cougars sometimes high up on the mountains."

I knew Jefferson Tidwell had settled in Wellington in 1879 two years after he married Sarah Seely. Wanting to know more I asked, "How old were your boys when they came here with you to mine coal?"

"They were pretty well grown by then." He laughed softly, "They were good boys and good workers, but they were glad when the Pleasant Valley Coal Company bought the rights from us the next year. Mining alone up here was hard work."

"Pleasant Valley? I thought it was the Utah Fuel Company?"

"T'was the same. The company just changed its name. Just like this valley. This was called the Sunset District at first."

"Did any of you stay here and work for the company?"

"They offered jobs to all of us who wanted to stay here. In fact, Frank built the first log cabin here and it was later enlarged to fit the whole family."

"Did you think the town would grow as fast as it did?"

"Well, you know, when they began work on the railroad here in 1899, and more mules were bought and more men were hired, I figured it wouldn't be long before the town grew. The miners wanted their families with them and the tents the company put up for them to live in were soon replaced with wood frame or rock houses." He looked around then went on, "The company built houses as fast as they could. See that hill up there across the way?"

I nodded.

"They built stone houses right up that hill. It was called Goblers Knob.

The trouble was they couldn't get enough water pressure up to those houses so the people had to carry their water in buckets from the taps at the foot of the hill up all those hundred steps." He laughed, "Course we didn't use water like you people do these days. We got by with a lot less."

"My parents told me about that. They lived up on Goblers Knob when Dean and Winifred were little. But, by the time I came along, there was nothing left of those houses but their foundations and all those steps."

Jefferson said quietly, "Yes, I've seen a lot of changes over the years. I saw Sunnyside grow and boom during two World Wars. And I saw it decline and deteriorate until there's nothing left but that chain link fence running up the valley and that bridge over there." He sighed, "I've been gone a long time but I can tell you this was a good place to live."

"I know," I said slowly, "I loved this old town. And I'm sorry it's gone now. I would have loved to bring my kids and grandkids here to see it." I started to rise, "But now I'd better start home."

I turned to say goodbye but there was no one there. I dusted myself off then hiked back down the mountain.

As I left the old Sunnyside townsite I looked once again at the sheep and thought, "This place has come full circle. The old Sunset District is turning back to nature's creatures."

As I drove home that evening I thought that the Sunnyside I knew as a boy will always live on, as long as there is one person left whose roots are there. One person who will take a child on his knee and with very special reverence, begin a conversation with, "When I was a boy . . .

I'll Be There

by Glen Turnerr

When I am gone from the world we know
And the seasons come and pass
And the years roll down to wherever they go
And memories stir in the wind-ruffled grass
Of deserts wide 'neath the cedar trees
Under the red-rock rim,
And clouds float by in the bluest sky—
Blue and white designs through the pinion pines
And the lattice of cedar limbs.
If you stand on the slope of a sage-covered hill
With the sun and the wind in your hair
And look out and down at the scrub-oak brush,
You know that I'll be there.

For I am a part of them and they are a part of me
In the patterns of life's design.
They have colored the threads in my pattern of life
In the tapestry of time.

The deserts, the mountains, the hills and the sea—
And the long road through the years—
Wherever you go on the roads we know—
They are all a part of me.

If you pause to enjoy the sunset's glow
As it softens a day of care,
As the colors fade in the evening shade
You know that I'll be there.

*(Our cousin Glen wrote this October 8, 1984 on the road between
Wellington and Woodside just north of the junction with the road to the
Horse Canyon mine.)*

DREAMING OF SUNNYSIDE

by Joyce Erickson Duke

I'm dreaming of Sunnyside, home of my childhood days.
In my dreaming I live again those golden yesterdays.
I'm walking a shady street, everyone says, "hello."
When I want to get away, to Sunnyside I go.
Long before microwave ovens; long before color TV;
when mothers knew all the neighbors, and cooked for the
     family.
Long before men burned their draft cards; long before
     superbowl fame;
back when soldiers were heroes, and football was just a
     game.
I'm dreaming of Sunnyside; I am a child once more,
in the swing daddy hung for us just outside the door.
I hear my dear mother's voice calling me inside.
But I just smile cause I realize I'm dreaming of
     Sunnyside.
Gone are the church and the schoolhouse;
Gone are the houses and trees.
But Sunnyside lives in our pictures, and in our memories.
I'm dreaming of Sunnyside, home of my childhood days.
In my dreaming I live again those golden yesterdays.
When the world closes in on me, and I want to run and
     hide,
I escape inside myself, dreaming of Sunnyside.
I escape inside myself, dreaming of Sunnyside,
just dreaming of Sunnyside.

The Second Reason For Writing

The second reason for writing this book is to show you that anyone can write a similar story about their life. If I can do it, you can do it too.

Don't put it off any longer. Your story needs to be written. Do it now. And, by the way, call me when your story is finished. If I'm still around I'd like to get a copy.

Book Price: $13.00 Shipping $3
Village Marketing
145 W 400 North
Richfield, Utah 84701

1-800-982-6683

Ten or more books: Call or write for discounts.